Joanne Weir's
COOKING
CONFIDENCE

Joanne Weir's
COOKING
CONFIDENCE

DINNER MADE SIMPLE

Joanne Weir

The Taunton Press

to my parents, with love

The Taunton Press
Inspiration for hands-on living®

The Taunton Press, Inc., 63 South Main Street,
PO Box 5506, Newtown, CT 06470-5506
e-mail: tp@taunton.com

Editor: Carolyn Mandarano
Copy editor: Nina Rynd Whitnah
Indexer: Heidi Blough
Jacket/Cover design: Laura Palese
Interior design: Laura Palese
Layout: Laura Palese
Photographer: Erin Kunkel
Food stylist: Erin Quon
Prop stylist: Ethel Brennan
Kitchen assistant: Karen Alvey
Hair and makeup: Nicole Sofios
The following names/manufacturers appearing in
Joanne Weir Cooking Confidence are trademarks:
Aperol®, Bob's Red Mill®, Kahlúa®, Maldon®,
Microplane®, Pernod®

Library of Congress Cataloging-in-Publication Data
in progress

ISBN: 978-1-60085-713-3

Printed in the United States of America
10 9 8 7 6 5 4 3 2 1

acknowledgments

This book is one I have always wanted to write and the companion to a television series I have longed to do, so it is with great pleasure that I see this dream come true. It is here that I hope to thank everyone who has played a very special role in bringing these things life.

First and foremost, a big thanks to my agent and dear friend, Doe Coover. I am happy we found a good home for *Joanne Weir's Cooking Confidence* with Taunton Press. A very special thanks to my editor, Carolyn Mandarano, whose patience, vision, and perceptive talent made this book a reality. I also want to thank Alison Wilkes for her art direction, Carol Singer, design manager, and Erin Giunta, for her photo editing.

I spent a good amount of time in my kitchen during the book's photo shoot with Erin Kunkel, the photographer, Erin Quon, food stylist, and Ethel Brennan, prop stylist. They all threw their hearts and creative talents into this project, and I am most grateful to them for their dedication.

Inken Chrisman was my shining star throughout this book project. She helped me with the proposal, brainstormed recipe ideas with me, and helped with writing and editing. I would also like to thank my assistant, Karen Alvey, for her superb recipe testing. She threw herself 100 percent into this book and then some! What a great friend and cheerleader! And a big kiss and thanks to my best wine pal and wine-business partner, Tim McDonald, for his wine, savvy, pairings, and expertise.

Now let's talk indebtedness... Paul Swensen, my TV husband, couldn't be a better friend, producer, director, and editor. We've worked together doing television since day one. His dedication, hard work, and utmost support turned a television career into an incredibly pleasurable journey. I thank my lucky stars to have Paul in my life!

And then there's the rest of the *Joanne Weir Cooking Confidence* TV crew. First and foremost, thanks to Sally Cohen, who devoted tireless hours collecting students, props, and products. Also thanks to Tim Bellan, whose keen eye never makes anything look "clunky and mechanical." You always make me shine and I thank you from my heart! Thanks to my culinary director, Chris Styler, and his extraordinary team, Andrea Boje and Karen Alvey. A big kiss to Amy Vogler, Nicole Sofios, Steve Bellan, Alan Hereford, Greg Peterson, Dean Miller, Kris Ravetto, Jason Gittens, Aurielle Perlmann, and Tony Jensen. Hats off to Hope Reed for great carriage, Gene Kinsella and ROK Media for fundraising efforts, Ryan and Heejung of Pixel by Inch for web design, and John Lawrence for his musical talent. Thanks to Lisa Landi, Mike Kahn, and everyone at KQED, as well as all the hard-working folks at American Public Television and CREATE Television, especially Jamie Haines. And thanks to all of my students on the show—I hope I've given you a little confidence in the kitchen.

This TV show and book wouldn't be possible without the support of my funders, Legends from Europe, U.S. Highbush Blueberry Council, Village Harvest, Meyer Cookware, Culinapp, and Valley Fig. A special thanks to Bob Huntley, Geoffrey Drummond, Chris Howard, Traci Ayer, and Dianne Hummel at Culinapp for producing the gorgeous app that accompanies the show.

I could never do what I have done this last year without my husband, Joe. I wrote a new cookbook, opened a restaurant, was executive producer of a TV series, and launched Joanne Weir Wines. You said I could do it, you gave me the confidence, and I love you for that.

contents

INTRODUCTION: DINNER MADE SIMPLE 2

dinner made simple

You may think that after having written 16 cookbooks, number 17 would be next to impossible to pull off. How could I possibly have anything more to share? Believe it or not, this book was the easiest for me to write because the inspiration is near and dear to my heart.

Teaching people to cook and inspiring confidence in the kitchen is the best part of my job. As host of the PBS cooking show *Joanne Weir's Cooking Confidence*, I've watched a ballet dancer whip eggs whites for a soufflé for the first time, a 10-year-old girl beam with pride while tasting a delicious lamb stew she's prepared, and newlyweds learn to make a tagine. This book showcases how I cook at home—and how so many of you want to cook for yourselves, your friends, and your family. With this book in hand, you, too, can step into your kitchen and make a fabulous dinner.

But let's face it—deciding what to eat for dinner is tough no matter who you are. We think about it every day. Even as a professional chef, I struggle with the dinner dilemma nightly. I'm incredibly busy every day. This year, I launched my own wine label, Joanne Weir Wines; opened my first restaurant, Copita (in Sausalito, California); created an iPad app; premiered my new cooking show, *Joanne Weir's Cooking Confidence*; and

started an online retail store via Open Sky. That's on top of my usual cooking classes, culinary tours in the Mediterranean, writing magazine articles, and being named Consulting Editor at Large for *Fine Cooking* magazine. By the end of each day, I'm spent. But the question of what's for dinner still lingers.

Like me, you're probably living a full-plate life. Regardless of whether you're juggling family, a career, or both, you're busy—and what to make for dinner can become a stressful end to what's already been a packed day. I'm here to help. Tackling the dinner challenge boils down to a simple mind shift and a few new habits. It involves being flexible in the kitchen, working with versatile ingredients, and shopping intelligently so that you have basic staples on hand at any given time. It also involves learning basic cooking techniques that can be used to create and then re-create healthy, fresh, affordable, and delicious home-cooked dinners.

BUILDING CONFIDENCE IN THE KITCHEN

First and foremost is the confidence factor. Many of my students enter the kitchen convinced they're going to "mess up" if they attempt something new. They shy away from dishes like risotto, soufflés, crêpes, and homemade pizza because they're convinced they can't do it. But as soon as they actually give it a shot, they realize that there was no reason to be intimidated.

Although I can't host each and every one of you in my home for a cooking lesson, I've done the next best thing. I've wrapped up all the confidence-building tips and tricks for making delicious home-cooked meals into this book. With this book by your side, it will be like having me there in your kitchen, whispering in your ear, encouraging you, guiding you, and teaching you how to become a better cook.

For recipes that involve a basic cooking skill that may appear to be intimidating, I've included "In the Kitchen" tips to teach you those skills. Whether it's figuring out if your skirt steak is cooked properly for Grilled Skirt Steak with Chimichurri or whipping egg whites to perfection for a Baby Spinach and Gruyère Soufflé, I'm with you every step of the way, instilling confidence in your kitchen abilities.

What you'll quickly come to realize is that the skills you're developing are transferrable from recipe to recipe. Not only will you have walked away with a kitchen skill that can be applied to many different recipes, but with skills in hand, you'll likely feel more comfortable experimenting with different flavor combinations for a dish. For example, let's say you try the Quick Risotto with Shrimp & Meyer Lemon (p. 75) one night (and master making risotto beautifully); next time, try a different flavor combination, like wild mushroom and blue cheese or fresh spring vegetables and mint. When you make the Spanish Lamb Stew with Smoked Paprika, Tomatoes & White Beans (p. 208), you'll learn all about browning meat and vegetables, adding stock, and simmering, which is the basis for making stew of any kind. The more you cook and experiment in the kitchen, the more you build your cooking repertoire and the easier and more fun cooking becomes.

BECOMING A SMART SHOPPER

While building your cooking repertoire and honing your skills are vital to building confidence in the kitchen, you also need to learn how to shop to make the most of your budget and time. This book is full of recipes for quick, delicious dinners on a budget.

How do I make sure my meals don't break the bank? I start by buying less-expensive cuts of meat without compromising flavor. Our mothers knew how to do it when they made pot roast, meat loaf, and sausages with beans. Then I select techniques like braising and slow cooking that show off these cuts of meat, which are typically tough unless they're cooked for a good length of time. Some people call it peasant food; I call it sensible, affordable dinner that's healthy for your waistline and wallet.

But there's another way to be a smart shopper—look for ingredient alternatives. Let's take a quick trip to the grocery store. You're at the fish case when you spot first-of-the-season king salmon. Your mouth drops when you see the price: about $25 a pound. Ouch, not this week. Instead, opt for fresh cod, which is less than half that per pound.

Next, you find yourself at the poultry case. You see boneless, skinless chicken breasts next to boned, skin-on chicken thighs at a third of the price. What do you choose? Most likely you grab the chicken breasts for ease and, frankly, because it's what you normally buy. You have probably also heard that white meat of chicken breasts is healthier for you than dark meat of thighs. But not so fast! Without the skin, there's very little difference between them. So what you might give up for ease (having to remove the skin), you lose in flavor and you take a hit to your wallet. You can take the same approach at the meat counter; opt for the skirt steak over the filet mignon and you have a richly flavorful cut of meat for a fraction of the cost.

This is just the beginning. There are so many choices that lend themselves to versatility once you've mastered the concept and techniques needed. If you don't trust your instincts yet, you'll find more ideas throughout this book in "At the Market" tips. Pretty soon you won't stress about shopping for the exact ingredients called for in a recipe. You'll have enough experience and confidence to make substitutions that make your life easier. You can see how this works—the more you cook, the more confident you become. The more confident you become, the more enjoyable cooking becomes, leading you to cook even more. It just builds and builds. And better yet, being in the kitchen becomes something to look forward to rather than dread. The question of "What's for dinner?" becomes a more exciting statement of "I can't wait to cook tonight."

KEEPING A STOCKED, FLEXIBLE PANTRY

This all sounds well and good, but there's still the stress of planning and shopping for dinner. I have some thoughts on that, too. The secret here is to always maintain a well-stocked pantry and refrigerator (see The Basic Pantry sidebar on p. 7). There are a handful of versatile ingredients I always keep on hand that can be used to create a wide variety of dishes. That way, at the drop of a hat, I can make something interesting for dinner. All I really have to shop for is seasonal produce and proteins, like chicken, fish, or meat. (It's also smart, though, to keep a package of things like chicken thighs, pork butt, or sausages in the freezer so you always have a back-up plan.) In addition to The Basic Pantry, look for "In the Pantry" tips throughout the book for some specific ways to add variety to your dishes.

Here's an example of the flexible pantry in action. Last night I made Cod Braised with Leeks, Potatoes & Thyme (p. 152). Sounds divine, right? Here's how it went. I heated some store-bought chicken stock, added

some mustard and capers, and a couple sprigs of fresh thyme. I had an open bottle of Sauvignon Blanc so I added a splash. I lined the bottom of the pan with some thin slices of unpeeled fingerling potatoes, topped them with a couple of thinly sliced leeks, and sprinkled on kosher salt and a pinch of black pepper. I covered the pan, placed it over medium heat, and set the timer for 12 minutes.

In the meantime, I set the table and poured a couple glasses of that very same white wine. I uncovered the pan, topped the leeks with a couple cod fillets I'd gotten at the store earlier that day, added a few drops of lemon juice and a good grating of lemon zest. A little more salt and pepper, then the cover went back on the pan for another 5 minutes.

As I ladled the fish, vegetables, and heady juices into wide soup bowls, the aromas were intoxicating. The thyme and lemon zest with leeks and fresh cod were incredible. This delicious dinner for two took only 20 minutes to create from start to finish and cost just a little over $10.

It really is that simple. It's all about having a few simple cooking tricks up your sleeve and learning how to be flexible with ingredients. I could have made a similar (and just as delicious) dish if I'd had salmon and fennel on hand instead of the cod and leeks. In case you're not yet convinced, here are a few more dinners I could easily toss together with what I have in my pantry: Rigatoni with Chicken, Tomatoes & Cream (chicken thighs in the freezer, pasta and canned tomatoes in the pantry, and cream in the fridge); Soft Polenta with Tomatoes, Sausage & Peppers (sausage in the freezer, polenta and tomatoes in the pantry, peppers from the market); Honey-Glazed Pork Chops with Orange & Cardamom (buy the meat from the market, orange in the fridge, spices in the pantry). Pretty incredible, huh? We're not talking bland, boring food. This is wow-factor food.

GETTING STARTED

Cooking is fun, and sharing a delicious dinner you've made with family and friends is something you can be proud of. Many of the dishes in this book are designed to be accessible and appropriate for a weeknight meal. But there are also a few recipes for dishes that take a little longer to prepare—but are just as easy to make—and are more suited to a Saturday night dinner party.

The recipes I've provided are for main courses, the first line of defense for home cooks. But every recipe also offers simple side dish, dessert, and wine recommendations so you can put together a full meal for yourself or when serving company. Your family and friends will think you spent hours in the kitchen and broke the bank shopping at 20 different stores. Let them. It'll be our little secret.

That's what *Joanne Weir's Cooking Confidence* is all about. Inspiring confidence in the kitchen by providing an assortment of easy, affordable, flexible, approachable, uncomplicated recipes for dinners that will blow you away. I often say I have the best job in the world because I get to share my love of food with others, traveling the globe to teach eager students how to cook. With this book, I hope to broaden my reach and continue to inspire even more magical moments of confidence in the kitchen.

the basic pantry

Keeping a well-stock pantry is one of the tricks to pulling together a delicious dinner quickly. Here are the things I almost always have on hand. While you don't necessarily need to have one of each of these items, be sure to have a selection from each category.

DRY PANTRY

Extra-virgin olive oil

Red-wine vinegar

White-wine vinegar

Balsamic vinegar

Soy sauce

Dijon mustard

Grainy mustard

Anchovies

Capers

Unbleached all-purpose flour

Bread flour

Panko

Semolina

Cornstarch

Brown sugar

Granulated sugar

Honey

Prepared harissa

Canned tomatoes (whole San Marzano and diced tomatoes)

Tomato paste

Canned beans (garbanzo and cannellini)

Dry white wine (Sauvignon Blanc)

Low-sodium chicken stock

Clam juice

Dry pasta

Dried beans (cannellini, garbanzo, pinto, and black beans)

Couscous

Brown rice

Basmati or jasmine rice

Polenta

Quinoa

FROZEN

Bread (for homemade breadcrumbs)

Chicken thighs

Pork sausage

Ground beef

Shrimp

REFRIGERATED & PRODUCE

Parmigiano-Reggiano

Greek yogurt

Garlic

Yellow onion

Fresh ginger

Lemons

Parsley

Olives

SPICES

Red pepper flakes

Coriander

Cumin

Cardamom

Fennel

Cayenne

Smoked paprika (pimentón)

Paprika

Ancho chile

Chile powder

Oregano

Ground cinnamon

Cloves

Bay leaves

Ginger

Turmeric

1

EAT YOUR
vegetables

THE RECIPES

TECHNIQUES MADE SIMPLE

bread salad with summer beans & feta

6 ounces coarse-textured rustic bread, 3 to 4 days old

Kosher salt and freshly ground black pepper

½ pound green beans, cut into 1-inch pieces

½ pound yellow wax beans, cut into 1-inch pieces

3 medium red tomatoes, seeded and cut into ¾-inch dice

3 medium yellow tomatoes, seeded and cut into ¾-inch dice

1 small red onion, cut into ½-inch dice

¼ cup fresh basil leaves, lightly packed

1 Tbs. coarsely chopped fresh oregano

5 Tbs. red-wine vinegar

⅓ cup extra-virgin olive oil

2 cloves garlic, minced

12 ounces feta cheese, coarsely crumbled

serves 6

POPULAR IN ITALY, PANZANELLA IS A REFRESHING SALAD MADE with leftover bread and tomatoes. Eating it always takes me back to Tuscany. I love teaching my students to make this simple dish, virtually transporting them to the rolling Tuscan hillsides. Here I've changed the classic a bit by adding green beans and yellow wax beans. I also like using feta cheese in panzanella. Although it's not a classic Italian cheese, it adds a wonderful salty quality to the salad. Give this recipe a try the next time you find yourself with leftover stale bread.

1. Slice the bread into 1-inch slices. Sprinkle with ½ cup water and let sit for 2 minutes. Carefully squeeze the bread until dry. Tear it into 1-inch pieces and let rest on paper towels for 20 minutes.

2. Bring a large saucepan of salted water to a boil. Add the green and yellow beans and simmer until tender but still crisp, 3 to 5 minutes. Drain and cool.

3. Place the tomatoes, onions, bread, and cooled green and yellow beans in a large serving bowl. Tear the basil into ½-inch pieces and toss carefully into the bowl along with the oregano.

4. In a small bowl, whisk together the vinegar, oil, and garlic. Season with salt and pepper. Carefully toss the salad with the vinaigrette and let rest for 20 minutes. Serve with the crumbled feta on top.

SERVING SUGGESTIONS

- Wine pairing: Sauvignon Blanc
- Serve with a bowl of gazpacho.
- For a simple dessert, slice fresh strawberries, drizzle with good-quality port, and sprinkle with freshly ground black pepper.

AT THE MARKET choosing bread

Making this salad is a good way to save a few pennies. Look for bread on the day-old rack at the market. Be sure to choose bread that's coarse textured, though. Light, airy bread just won't work here.

baked crêpes with creamy mushrooms & prosciutto

½ ounce dried wild mushrooms

6 Tbs. unsalted butter, plus more for the pan

1 medium yellow onion, minced

½ pound fresh button mushrooms, thinly sliced

6 ounces thinly sliced prosciutto, cut into thin strips

2 Tbs. unbleached all-purpose flour

2 cups milk

¾ cup grated Parmigiano-Reggiano

Kosher salt and freshly ground black pepper

1 recipe Crêpes (recipe on p. 15)

2 Tbs. dry homemade breadcrumbs

makes 12 crêpes; serves 6

CRÊPES HAVE A REPUTATION FOR BEING A CULINARY CHALLENGE. The misconceptions are that the lacy French pancakes are too delicate to flip, or that you'll be a slave to the stove as you work to turn out crêpes serving by serving. Neither is the case in this recipe. The batter makes crêpe making easy, and you can even make the crêpes a day in advance! The best part? The crêpes are folded around a beautiful, creamy mushroom filling and layered in a baking dish, so dinner comes together in one fell swoop.

1. Pour 2 cups of boiling water over the dried mushrooms and let sit for 30 minutes. Drain and reserve the water. Chop the mushrooms coarsely and set aside. If the mushroom water is sandy, filter it through a paper-towel-lined strainer; set aside.

2. Heat 2 Tbs. of butter in a frying pan over medium heat. Add the onions and cook, stirring occasionally, until soft, about 7 minutes. Add the fresh mushrooms and continue to cook, stirring occasionally, until the mushrooms have evaporated their liquid, 10 minutes. Add the chopped wild mushrooms and continue to cook for 1 minute. Add the reserved mushroom water, turn the heat to high, and simmer, stirring constantly, until almost dry, 10 minutes. Turn the heat to medium, add the prosciutto, and continue to cook for 2 minutes.

3. Melt 3 Tbs. of butter in a saucepan over low heat. Add the flour and stir constantly for 2 minutes. Add the milk, stirring constantly, and cook until the mixture thickens, 2 to 3 minutes. Add the mushroom-prosciutto mixture and mix well. Add ½ cup of Parmigiano-Reggiano and season with salt and pepper.

4. Heat the oven to 425°F. Butter the bottom and sides of a 9 x 12-inch baking dish.

continued on p. 14

- Wine pairing: Pinot Noir or Pinot Gris
- Start dinner with a butter lettuce salad with shaved radishes and green goddess dressing.
- For dessert, slightly soften some store-bought vanilla ice cream. Place it in a bowl and quickly stir in toasted sliced almonds and hand-chopped bittersweet chocolate to make chocolate almond crunch ice cream. Refreeze until firm, then serve.

5. Place a crêpe flat on the work surface. Spread half of it with a few tablespoons of filling. Fold in half, then quarters, forming a triangle. Stand the triangles in the baking dish so the curved side is up and the crêpes are overlapping one another. Repeat with the remaining crêpes and filling. Melt the remaining 1 Tbs. butter and brush on the tops of the crêpes. Combine the remaining ¼ cup grated Parmigiano-Reggiano and the breadcrumbs. Sprinkle over the top. Bake the crêpes until golden on top, about 20 minutes.

IN THE KITCHEN making crêpes

Crêpes are not hard to make once you get the hang of it. It's all about getting the right consistency of the batter and then quickly swirling the batter in the hot crêpe pan to coat the bottom. A little practice makes perfect crêpes.

Crêpe batter needs to flow smoothly but shouldn't be runny.

To flip a crêpe, use a thin-blade spatula to lift the crêpe, and use your fingers to pull it out of the pan gently and flip it over.

crêpes

2 cups unbleached all-purpose flour

Kosher salt

1¾ cups milk

4 eggs

4 to 5 Tbs. unsalted butter

makes 12 crêpes

1. Put the flour and ½ tsp. salt in a bowl and add the milk slowly, a little at a time, mixing vigorously with a fork to avoid lumps. Add 1 egg at a time, beating rapidly with a fork after each addition. Let the batter rest for 30 minutes.

2. Grease the bottom of an 8-inch crêpe pan with 1 tsp. of butter. Place the pan over medium heat. Stir the batter, pour ⅓ cup into the pan, and rotate the pan to completely cover the bottom. As soon as the batter has set (45 to 60 seconds), loosen the crêpe with a spatula and flip the crêpe. When the other side is firm, remove the crêpe from the pan and place it on a plate. Repeat with the rest of the batter, stirring the batter occasionally and adding butter to the pan if the crêpes begin to stick. The crêpes can be stacked on top of one another until ready to use.

couscous feast with five vegetables & caramelized onions

4 Tbs. unsalted butter

2 tsp. ginger powder

3 cinnamon sticks

1 tsp. turmeric

½ tsp. saffron threads

Kosher salt and freshly ground black pepper

10 sprigs fresh cilantro, tied together with kitchen string

3 Tbs. tomato paste

4 yellow onions, thinly sliced

1 tsp. ground cinnamon

½ cup honey

½ cup raisins

5 carrots, peeled and halved

1 large turnip, peeled and cut into 1½-inch chunks

½ head green cabbage, cut into eighths

1 small butternut or turban squash, unpeeled, halved, seeded, and cut into 2-inch pieces

1 pound zucchini, cut into 1½-inch pieces

2 cups dry couscous (about 14 ounces)

2 tsp. harissa

serves 6 to 8

THIS VEGETARIAN COUSCOUS PLATTER IS TRULY A FEAST. THE LIGHT, fluffy North African semolina pasta provides a nest for tender vegetables, which have simmered in bold stock seasoned with ginger, cinnamon, turmeric, saffron, cilantro, and tomato paste. The onions, caramelized with honey, cinnamon, and raisins, melt in your mouth and serve as the perfect counterpart to the savory vegetables.

This dish is wonderful when entertaining. Serve the colorful platter with two pitchers of the seasoned vegetable stock alongside, one mild and one spiked with smoky harissa, a North African hot chile sauce. Your guests may choose which stock to drizzle atop their individual serving.

1. Place 2 Tbs. of butter, the ginger, cinnamon sticks, turmeric, saffron, 1½ tsp. salt, ½ tsp. pepper, the tied cilantro sprigs, tomato paste, and 10 cups water in a large soup pot. Bring to a boil over medium-high heat. Reduce the heat to medium low and simmer for 20 minutes.

2. In the meantime, make the caramelized onions. Place the onions in a large frying pan with 2 cups water over medium high heat. Cover and cook for 10 minutes. Remove the cover and drain the onions. Discard the water. Transfer 1 cup of the stock from the soup pot to the onions and add the ground cinnamon, honey, and raisins. Reduce the heat to medium low. Cover and cook until the onions are very soft, 30 minutes. Uncover and cook until the onions are almost dry, about 5 minutes. Season with salt; set aside.

3. Add the carrots, turnip pieces, cabbage, and squash to the stock and simmer for 10 minutes. Add the zucchini and cook until all of the vegetables are tender, 5 minutes.

4. In a large saucepan, bring 3½ cups water and 1 tsp. salt to a boil. Add the couscous, stir well, remove from the heat, and let it sit, covered, for 5 minutes.

5. To serve, remove 2 cups of the stock from the soup pot and place in a pitcher. In another pitcher, put 2 cups of stock from the soup pot and add the harissa to taste.

6. Dump the hot couscous on a large platter and fluff. Dot with the remaining 2 Tbs. butter and toss to melt the butter. Moisten the couscous with a few ladles of stock from the soup pot. Make a well in the center and place the vegetables in the center. Top with the onions. Serve immediately with both pitchers of stock.

SERVING SUGGESTIONS

- Wine pairing: Riesling
- For this celebratory feast, start with a citrus salad topped with mint and red onions.

- For dessert, serve hot Moroccan mint tea and cookies.

farfalle with corn, summer squash, peas & basil oil

1 cup fresh basil leaves

10 fresh spearmint leaves

½ cup extra-virgin olive oil

4 ears of sweet corn

1 cup very coarse fresh breadcrumbs

Kosher salt

12 ounces farfalle pasta

1½ pounds summer squash, cut into ¾-inch dice

1½ cups English peas (fresh or frozen)

2 tsp. freshly grated lemon zest

1 Tbs. freshly squeezed lemon juice

Freshly ground black pepper

serves 6

YOU'RE GOING TO FALL HEAD OVER HEELS IN LOVE WITH THIS PASTA dish. It's light and fresh and perfectly showcases the sweetness of summertime produce. The basil oil, which coats the homemade breadcrumbs and serves as a sauce for the pasta itself, is so bright and refreshing that I'm tempted to eat it by the spoonful. Adding just a handful of spearmint leaves to the basil oil somehow intensifies the basil flavor. Not sure what I mean? Try it. And don't skip the finishing touch—topping the farfalle with breadcrumbs, which adds just the right amount of crunch to an already spectacular dish.

1. Heat an oven to 375F° and place an oven rack in the center of the oven.

2. Bring a pot of water to a boil. Add the basil and mint leaves and blanch for 10 seconds. Remove with a slotted spoon and rinse immediately under cold water. Drain well, pat dry, and place in a blender or food processor and purée. With the motor running, slowly add the oil and process until smooth, about 30 seconds.

3. In the meantime, fill a large frying pan (large enough to fit the corn) with water and bring to a boil. Add the corn and simmer, turning occasionally, until the kernels turn a slightly darker yellow on all sides, 5 to 6 minutes. Remove from the water and let cool. Break each ear of corn in half and cut the kernels of corn off the cob (see p. 41). Discard the cobs and reserve the kernels.

4. Place the breadcrumbs on a baking sheet. Drizzle with 2 Tbs. of basil oil and toss the crumbs to distribute the oil evenly. Season with salt and bake, tossing occasionally, until the crumbs turn golden brown, 10 to 15 minutes. Remove from the oven and let cool.

5. About 10 minutes before serving, bring a large pot of salted water to a boil. Add the farfalle and cook until al dente, 10 minutes, or according to the package instructions.

- Wine pairing: Arneis
- My favorite comfort soup—Pasta Brodo, homemade chicken stock with pastina and lots of grated Parmigiano-Reggiano—is a wonderful accompaniment to this dish.
- For dessert, toss an assortment of summer berries with Cassis and top with softly whipped cream.

6. In the meantime, warm 2 Tbs. of basil olive oil in a large frying pan over medium heat. Add the squash and cook until it begins to soften, 3 minutes. Add the corn and peas and cook until the corn and peas are warm, 1 minute. Add the remaining basil oil and toss together.

7. When the farfalle is done cooking, drain, saving 2 Tbs. of the pasta water. Put the pasta back in the pot and toss with the pasta water, vegetables, lemon zest, and lemon juice. Season with salt and pepper to taste. Place in a large serving bowl and top with the breadcrumbs. Serve immediately.

IN THE KITCHEN making breadcrumbs

To make homemade breadcrumbs, you can either buy a fresh loaf of white bread or use up leftover bread.

Place the bread in a food processor (cut off the crusts first, if you like) and process until you have a fine crumb. To toast breadcrumbs, spread the crumbs on a baking sheet and bake in a 350°F oven, tossing occasionally, until dry and light golden, 10 to 12 minutes.

If you have leftover breadcrumbs, put them in a zip-top bag and store in the freezer for later use.

fettuccine with asparagus ribbons & lemon crème fraîche

2 pounds asparagus

Kosher salt

2 cups low-sodium chicken stock

1 cup crème fraîche

1 tsp. freshly grated lemon zest

1 tsp. freshly squeezed lemon juice

12 ounces dry fettuccine

1½ cups finely grated Parmigiano-Reggiano

serves 6

WITH ITS LONG, SLENDER SPEARS AND FLOWERING HEAD, ASPARAGUS is the most beautiful sign that spring has sprung. In this recipe, I maintain the integrity of the asparagus by thinly shaving the spears lengthwise with a vegetable peeler. The delicate wisps perfectly mirror the fettuccine for a dish that is equally stunning and delicious. Tossed with the steaming hot fettuccine at the end, the asparagus maintains its texture and superfresh flavor. When buying dry fettuccine, make sure you buy 100% semolina pasta.

1. Cut 2 inches of the tips off the asparagus and cut those pieces diagonally into ½-inch pieces. Bring a pot of salted water to a boil and boil the asparagus pieces until almost tender and bright green, 2 minutes. Drain immediately and set aside.

2. With the remaining asparagus spears, shave as much of the asparagus as you can with a vegetable peeler and reserve the shavings in a bowl (see the sidebar on p. 22). Coarsely cut the remaining centers of the asparagus and place them in a saucepan with the chicken stock. Place over medium heat and simmer until the asparagus is very tender and pale colored and only ½ cup of chicken stock remains, 15 to 20 minutes.

3. In a small bowl, combine the crème fraîche, lemon zest, and lemon juice and season with salt. Reserve.

4. Bring a large pot of salted water to a boil. Add the pasta and cook until al dente, 8 to 12 minutes, or according to the package instructions. Drain immediately and place in a large bowl. Add the shaved asparagus, cooked asparagus tips, chicken stock with asparagus, and a handful of Parmigiano-Reggiano. Toss together.

5. Serve immediately garnished with a sprinkling of Parmigiano-Reggiano and a dollop of crème fraîche. Serve the remaining Parmigiano separately at the table.

continued on p. 22

- Wine pairing: Sauvignon Blanc or Prosecco

- For a first course, toast some bread and top it with goat cheese, lemon zest, and a pinch of salt. Take a handful of sugar snap peas and simmer them just until tender, 1 minute. Top the goat cheese with the sugar snaps and a chiffonade (or thin strips) of fresh mint.

- End the meal with a bowl of orange sorbet topped with orange sections and a drizzle of Grand Marnier.

IN THE KITCHEN ## making asparagus ribbons

Working on a cutting board or work surface, hold one spear of asparagus in your left hand (if you're a righty; hold it in your right hand if you're a lefty). With your other hand, shave the asparagus into thin ribbons with a vegetable peeler.

eggplant parmigiana

2 Tbs. extra-virgin olive oil, plus more for brushing the pan and eggplant

1 small red onion, left whole, peeled

5 cups tomatoes, peeled, seeded, and diced (fresh or canned)

3 Tbs. tomato paste

1 tsp. sugar

1 small bunch fresh basil

Kosher salt and freshly ground black pepper

2 eggplants (about 2 pounds), peeled and cut into ¼-inch slices

12 ounces mozzarella, coarsely grated

1½ cups grated Parmigiano-Reggiano

serves 6 to 8

SERVING SUGGESTIONS

- Wine pairing: Chianti
- Start your dinner with roasted red pepper soup.
- Serve dinner with a loaf of warmed crusty bread and olive oil for dipping.
- For dessert, serve grilled halved peaches with honey and mascarpone.

I LOVE A GOOD EGGPLANT PARMIGIANA, BUT ALL TOO OFTEN I SEE the eggplant caked in heavy breading, which ultimately turns into a big gloppy mess. In this version, I let the pleasant bitterness and unique spongy texture of the eggplant shine. The eggplant is brushed with olive oil, baked until light golden brown, then layered with a simple homemade tomato sauce, fresh basil, and Parmigiano-Reggiano and mozzarella. The result is a lighter, more delicate version of an Italian favorite.

1. Heat the oven to 375°F.

2. Heat the oil in a large pot over medium-high heat. Add the onion, tomatoes, 2 cups water, the tomato paste, and sugar. With the back of a chef's knife, tap four basil sprigs to release the juices. Add the basil and salt and pepper to taste to the pot and bring to a boil. Reduce the heat to low and simmer until approximately 3 to 3½ cups of the mixture remains, about 30 to 45 minutes. Remove the basil sprigs and onion and discard. Purée the tomato sauce in a blender until smooth.

3. In the meantime, brush a baking sheet liberally with oil. Place the eggplant in a single layer on the baking sheet and brush the tops of the eggplant liberally with oil. Season with salt. Bake, turning occasionally, until the eggplant is cooked and light golden brown on both sides, 20 to 30 minutes.

4. In a 9 x 13-inch baking dish, spread half of the tomato sauce to cover the bottom. Place half of the eggplant slices on top of the sauce. Tear several basil leaves into small pieces and scatter them over the eggplant. Sprinkle with half of the mozzarella and Parmigiano-Reggiano. Repeat layering with the remaining ingredients, ending with the cheeses.

5. Bake, uncovered, until golden brown and bubbling, about 30 minutes.

fried potato & spiced red pepper frittata

2 medium red bell peppers

2 medium baking potatoes, such as russet or Idaho

1¼ cups pure olive oil

5 eggs

Large pinch of crushed red pepper flakes

Kosher salt and freshly ground black pepper

1 tsp. white-wine vinegar

1 Tbs. extra-virgin olive oil

1 to 2 cups microgreens

serves 4 to 6

SERVING SUGGESTIONS

• Wine pairing: Brachetto

• Start with white bean and sausage soup.

• For dessert, grill pineapple and serve warm topped with vanilla ice cream.

THIS FRITTATA IS THE PERFECT EXAMPLE OF HOW THE SIMPLEST ingredients can create the most mouth-watering meal. Inspired by the Spanish tortilla española, this frittata combines eggs with potatoes, roasted red peppers, and red pepper flakes, all of which I keep on hand in my pantry. Two simple steps, pan-frying the potatoes in olive oil and roasting the red peppers over an open flame, add a depth of flavor that elevates the frittata above its basic ingredients.

You can see in this recipe I have used both pure and extra-virgin olive oil. There is a big difference. Extra-virgin olive oil is the first pressing of the olive and has a much more aromatic flavor. I use mostly extra-virgin olive oil and especially in a dish that isn't cooked. Here, I used pure olive oil for frying the potatoes for a lighter flavor.

1. Heat a gas grill on high. Roast the peppers by placing them directly on the grates; grill, rotating as needed, until all sides are charred and the skin is completely black, about 10 minutes. (See the sidebar on the facing page for other roasting options.) Put the peppers in a plastic bag, close tightly, and let cool for 10 minutes. With a small knife, remove the skin and seeds, then cut the peppers into ½-inch dice.

2. Peel the potatoes. Cut approximately ½-inch slices but stop when halfway through the slice; turn and twist the knife so that the potato slices break off into very rough shapes or chips.

3. Heat the pure olive oil in an 8- to 9-inch, nonstick frying pan over medium heat and add the potatoes. There should be space between the potatoes because of the angles and the way they were cut. Cook the potatoes slowly, lifting and turning them occasionally, until they are tender but not brown.

4. Meanwhile, in a bowl, beat the eggs and crushed red pepper with salt and pepper to taste with a fork until they are slightly foamy.

5. Remove the potatoes from the frying pan and drain in a colander; reserve 3 Tbs. of the oil. Add the potatoes and roasted peppers to the

beaten eggs, pressing the potatoes down so they are completely covered by the egg. Let the mixture stand for 15 minutes.

6. Heat 2 Tbs. of reserved oil in a large frying pan until very hot. Turn the heat to medium low and add the potato and egg mixture, rapidly spreading it out in the frying pan with a spatula. Using a fork, loosen the edges and let the runny egg roll underneath. Continue to cook until the tortilla is almost set and the bottom is golden brown, 8 to 12 minutes. Invert a plate a little larger than the circumference of the pan onto the top of the pan and turn the tortilla onto the plate. Add the remaining 1 Tbs. of reserved oil to the pan and slide the tortilla back into the skillet. Cook until the tortilla is cooked through, 4 to 6 minutes. It should be slightly juicy inside.

7. In a bowl, whisk together the vinegar and extra-virgin olive oil. Season with salt and pepper. Toss with the microgreens.

8. Place the tortilla on a platter and cut into wedges. Top with the salad and serve hot or at room temperature.

IN THE KITCHEN roasting bell peppers

It's really easy to roast your own peppers, and there are three different ways to do it.

One way is to place a pepper directly on the grate of your stove's gas jets or on an outdoor gas grill. A second way is to cut bell peppers in half lengthwise, removing and discarding the stems, seeds, and ribs. Place the peppers cut side down on a baking sheet and broil until the skin is blackened, 6 to 10 minutes. The last method of roasting is to place the peppers on a baking sheet in a 500°F oven for 10 to 15 minutes, or until the skins are slightly wrinkled. With this method the skin doesn't turn black, though you will still be able to remove it from the flesh of the pepper.

Regardless of which method you choose, transfer the cooked peppers to a plastic bag and seal or place on the counter and cover with an inverted bowl. Either way creates a steam chamber, which will loosen skin of the pepper from the flesh. Let sit for 10 minutes.

Remove the skin by scraping with a knife. It's best not to run the steamed peppers under water or you will lose the smoky flavor.

green bean & potato salad with tahini & dukkah-dusted pitas

⅓ cup freshly squeezed lemon juice

¼ cup tahini paste

2 cloves garlic, minced

1 tsp. freshly grated lemon zest

¼ cup extra-virgin olive oil

Kosher salt and freshly ground black pepper

1 pound small red potatoes

½ pound green wax beans, ends trimmed, cut in half

8 cups salad greens

1 recipe Dukkah-Dusted Pitas (recipe on the facing page)

serves 6

DUKKAH IS A TRADITIONAL EGYPTIAN SIDE DISH MADE WITH NUTS, herbs, and spices. Here, a homemade pistachio and sesame seed dukkah is used to coat pita bread, which is then baked to create insanely delicious, crispy pita chips. Tossed into a mix of green beans, red potatoes, and greens with a lemon-tahini vinaigrette and we're talking about one killer salad. Want my advice? Make some extra dukkah-dusted pita chips just to snack on; otherwise, you won't have any left to add the perfect crunch to your salad. They're that good.

1. Make the dressing by whisking together the lemon juice, tahini, garlic, lemon zest, and oil. Season with salt and pepper.

2. Place a steamer basket in a large saucepan with an inch of water below. Bring the water to a boil over high heat and add the potatoes. Cover and steam until they can be skewered easily with a knife, 15 minutes. Remove the potatoes and when they are cool, cut into ¼-inch slices.

3. In the same steamer, add more water and bring the water to a boil. Add the green beans and cook until they're bright green and almost tender, 3 to 5 minutes. Drain and run under cold water.

4. To serve, toss the salad greens, potatoes, green beans, and pitas with the dressing and mound onto plates.

SERVING SUGGESTIONS

- Wine pairing: Riesling
- Start with a small platter of a piece of feta drizzled with olive oil, surrounded with Kalamata olives, roasted peppers, brined artichokes, and crostini.

- For dessert, serve a dollop of Greek yogurt drizzled with honey and topped with toasted pine nuts.

dukkah-dusted pitas

⅓ cup shelled pistachios

2 Tbs. sesame seeds

2 Tbs. coriander seeds

1½ Tbs. cumin seeds

1 tsp. fennel seeds

2 tsp. black peppercorns

1 tsp. dried oregano

Kosher salt

2 whole pita breads, 7 to 8 inches
in diameter

Extra-virgin olive oil, for brushing

makes 24 to 32

1. Heat a heavy frying pan over medium-high heat. Add the pistachios and cook, stirring frequently, for 4 minutes. Add the sesame seeds and cook, stirring frequently, until the sesame seeds are golden, 1 minute. Remove the pistachios and sesame seeds from the pan and place in a bowl.

2. Add the coriander, cumin, and fennel seeds and cook, stirring frequently, until aromatic, 30 to 45 seconds. Add to the bowl with the pistachios and sesame seeds. Add the peppercorns, oregano, and 1 tsp. salt to the bowl.

3. Place the mixture in a spice grinder and pulse a few times until the ingredients are the size of small breadcrumbs. Do not overprocess the dukkah.

4. Heat the oven to 375°F.

5. Cut the edges off the pita with scissors, and separate the pita into two rounds. Cut each round into 6 or 8 wedges. Place the pita wedges on a baking sheet in a single layer. Brush well with olive oil and dust the pitas with the dukkah. Bake in the oven, moving the wedges around so that none brown too quickly, until they are golden and crisp, 12 minutes.

grilled summer vegetable
sandwich with harissa aïoli

¼ cup extra-virgin olive oil

3 zucchini (about 10 ounces), cut into ¼-inch slices

1 eggplant (about 10 ounces), peeled and cut into ¼-inch slices

3 medium red peppers, quartered, cored, and seeded

Kosher salt and freshly ground black pepper

¾ cup mayonnaise

2 cloves garlic, minced

1½ tsp. sweet paprika

1 to 3 Tbs. harissa

12 slices rustic, coarse-textured bread

serves 6

SERVING SUGGESTIONS

• Drink pairing: Greco

• Serve the sandwiches with salt-and-vinegar potato chips.

• For dessert, serve homemade chocolate chip cookies.

A VEGETARIAN SANDWICH DOESN'T USUALLY GET MY HEART racing, but this one does. It's all about the spicy aïoli. Whether you start with homemade or store-bought mayo, give it a kick with plenty of garlic, sweet paprika, and harissa. The resulting smoky-hot and creamy condiment is all that's needed to take this sandwich to the next level. While you're at it, whip up some extra aïoli to enjoy with your next burger, turkey sandwich, or even steamed artichokes.

1. Heat an outdoor grill to medium-high heat.

2. Brush the olive oil liberally onto the zucchini and eggplant slices and the pepper quarters. Season with salt and pepper. Place the vegetables on the grill and cook until they're tender and light golden, 4 to 5 minutes for the zucchini, 10 to 12 minutes for the eggplant, and 8 to 10 minutes for the peppers. Remove from the grill and set aside.

3. Put the peppers in a zip-top bag and close tightly; let rest for about 10 minutes. Remove the peppers from the bag and with a small knife, remove the black skin and discard. Cut the pepper quarters in half.

4. In a small bowl, whisk the mayonnaise, garlic, paprika, and as much harissa as you like to make a spicy aïoli.

5. Toast the bread on both sides until golden. To assemble the sandwiches, spread half of the aïoli on 6 slices of the bread, distributing evenly. Top with the vegetables, distributing evenly. Spread the remaining aïoli on the remaining slices of bread and place on the top. Cut across diagonally into 2 pieces and serve immediately.

IN THE PANTRY harissa

Harissa is a spicy-hot condiment made in North Africa, mainly Morocco, Algeria, and Tunisia. You will find it in well-stocked grocery stores; it's available in either a tube or a can. I prefer buying it in a tube so that I can use what I need and store the remaining safely.

mushroom & blue cheese galette

FOR THE CRUST

1¼ cups unbleached all-purpose flour, chilled in the freezer for 1 hour

Kosher salt

8 Tbs. unsalted butter, cut into ½-inch pieces, chilled in the freezer for 1 hour

4 Tbs. sour cream

2 tsp. freshly squeezed lemon juice

½ cup ice water

FOR THE FILLING

¼ ounce dry porcini mushrooms

1 cup boiling water

2 Tbs. unsalted butter

6 green onions, white and green parts, thinly sliced

½ tsp. chopped fresh rosemary

½ tsp. chopped fresh thyme

1 pound cultivated or button mushrooms, thinly sliced

Kosher salt and freshly ground black pepper

4 ounces blue-veined cheese, such as Stilton, Gorgonzola, Maytag Blue, or Roquefort

serves 6

UMAMI IS COMMONLY REFERRED TO AS THE FIFTH TASTE, AFTER sweet, sour, bitter, and salty. It is a term used to describe flavor that is rich and savory, and has great depth—something that tastes so delicious that it makes you moan with delight. This galette—another name for a rustic tart—is chock full of umami, with dried porcinis, sautéed mushrooms, and blue cheese all nestled in a flaky, buttery crust. I dare you to try this without letting out a moan.

Make the crust

Place the flour and ½ tsp. salt in a food processor and pulse two times to combine. Add the butter and pulse several times until most of the mixture is the size of breadcrumbs with a few pieces the size of peas. Dump the mixture onto a work surface in a pile. Spread out the pile a little, and make a well in the center. Whisk together the sour cream, lemon juice, and water and add half of the liquid to the well. With your fingertips or a fork, mix the liquid with the dry ingredients until large lumps hold together. Remove the large lumps and repeat with the remaining liquid. Use as much of the liquid as needed to hold the dough together. Form the dough into a ball, cover with plastic wrap, and let rest in the refrigerator for 1 hour.

Make the filling

1. Heat the oven to 400°F. Place the dry porcini mushrooms in a small bowl, cover with the boiling water, and let sit for 30 minutes. Drain the mushrooms and reserve the liquid for another use. Finely mince the mushrooms and reserve.

2. Melt the butter in a large frying pan over medium heat. Add the green onions and cook, stirring occasionally, until soft, 5 minutes. Add the rosemary and thyme and continue to cook for 1 minute. Increase the heat to high, add the fresh and minced dried mushrooms, and cook until the mushrooms are soft and the liquid from the mushrooms has completely evaporated, 8 to 10 minutes. Remove from the pan and cool. Season with salt and pepper.

continued on p. 32

- Wine pairing: Dolcetto

- For an appetizer, make a simple bruschetta by toasting thinly sliced crusty bread on the grill, under the broiler, or in the toaster. Rub with a whole clove of peeled garlic. Brush with extra-virgin olive oil and sprinkle with Maldon® or sea salt. If you want to get fancy, omit the salt and top with a thin slice of prosciutto or a thin shaving of Manchego.

- Serve a green salad on the side of the galette.

- For dessert, drizzle warm chocolate sauce over mocha ice cream and top with roasted pecans.

Make the galette

1. Roll the dough on a floured surface to make a 12-inch circle. Place on a baking sheet. In a bowl, combine the blue cheese and mushrooms. Spread the mixture over the dough, leaving a 1½-inch border around the edge. Fold the uncovered edge of the pastry over the mushrooms and cheese, pleating it to make it fit and leaving a hole in the center of the tart. Bake until golden brown, 30 to 40 minutes. Let cool for 5 minutes, then slide the galette onto a serving plate. Serve hot, warm, or at room temperature.

IN THE KITCHEN why chill butter and flour?

Rather than spend hours in the kitchen making a classic puff pastry, I make this simple rough pastry dough. I like to freeze the butter and flour separately before making them into the dough. This way, when I roll out the dough, the frozen bits create layers; as the dough bakes, the butter melts between the layers and makes a very flaky pastry.

pepperoni pizza strata

4 cups cherry tomatoes

3 Tbs. extra-virgin olive oil

Kosher salt

8 large eggs

2 cups half-and-half

2 Tbs. chopped fresh basil

1 Tbs. chopped fresh oregano

Pinch of crushed red pepper flakes

½ pound stale artisanal bread, cut into 1-inch cubes (about 6 cups)

8 ounces fresh mozzarella, diced

3 ounces pepperoni, cut into ½-inch dice

¾ cup freshly grated Grana Padano or Parmigiano-Reggiano

serves 6

STRATA IS A DELICIOUS, SAVORY VERSION OF BREAD PUDDING. THIS recipe combines all of the things I love about pizza—oven-roasted tomatoes, pepperoni, basil, oregano, and cheesy goodness—without the need to mess with pizza dough. Using day-old artisanal bread and a savory egg-custard base, this dinner could not be easier or more satisfying.

1. Heat the oven to 400°F.

2. Place the tomatoes on a baking sheet and drizzle with 2 Tbs. of oil. Toss together and season with salt. Spread the tomatoes in a single layer and roast in the oven until the tomatoes are soft and most of the liquid from the tomatoes has evaporated, 20 to 25 minutes. Let cool for 10 minutes.

3. In a bowl, whisk together the eggs, half-and-half, basil, oregano, and crushed red pepper flakes. Add the bread, stir gently, and let sit for 5 minutes.

4. Add the tomatoes, mozzarella, pepperoni, and half of the Grana Padano or Parmigiano-Reggiano to the egg and bread mixture. With the remaining 1 Tbs. oil, grease a 2½-quart baking dish, then pour the mixture into the baking dish. Sprinkle the remaining cheese on top and bake until the strata has set and is golden on top, 25 to 30 minutes. Let rest for 5 minutes before serving.

SERVING SUGGESTIONS

- Wine pairing: Barbera or Nebbiolo
- Serve a Caesar salad alongside the strata.

- For dessert, drizzle 2 scoops of lemon sorbet with Limoncello.

skillet-baked eggs in piperade

3 Tbs. extra-virgin olive oil

4 ounces thinly sliced prosciutto, cut into ½-inch squares

2 red onions, halved and thinly sliced

3 garlic cloves, minced

2 Tbs. chopped fresh flat-leaf parsley

½ tsp. chopped fresh thyme

2 medium red bell peppers, halved, seeded, and cut into ¼-inch strips

2 medium green bell peppers, halved, seeded, and cut into ¼-inch strips

2½ cups tomatoes, peeled, seeded, and diced (fresh or canned)

2 tsp. piment d'Espelette

Kosher salt

6 large eggs

serves 6

NOWADAYS YOU'LL FIND EGGS ALL OVER THE PLACE—ON SALADS, atop burgers, in pasta, you name it. In this egg-centric dinner, inspired by my travels through Spain, they are baked in piperade, a classic Basque dish of onions, bell peppers, and tomatoes sautéed with piment d'Espelette pepper. The bright yellow, runny yolk adds a silky texture and rich flavor as it seeps into the nest of piperade. If you can't find piment d'Espelette, a combination of ⅛ tsp. cayenne and 1½ tsp. sweet paprika will work just as well.

1. Place a large frying pan over medium heat and add 1 Tbs. of oil. When the oil is shimmering, add the prosciutto and cook, stirring occasionally, until light golden, about 4 to 5 minutes. Remove with a slotted spoon and set aside.

2. Return the pan to medium heat and add the remaining 2 Tbs. oil. Add the onions and garlic and cook, stirring occasionally, until soft, about 10 minutes. Reduce the heat to medium low and add the parsley, thyme, and red and green peppers. Cover and cook, stirring occasionally, until the peppers are soft, 8 minutes.

3. Stir in the diced tomatoes, prosciutto, and piment d'Espelette and season well with salt. Cook, uncovered, until the piperade thickens slightly, 10 to 15 minutes. Taste and season as needed.

4. With a soup spoon, make 6 indentations in the piperade. Crack the eggs, one at a time, into the indentations. Do not stir. Cover the pan and cook until the egg whites are set but the yolks are still soft, 5 to 7 minutes.

5. With a large serving spoon, scoop out piperade with an egg, being sure not to crack the yolk, into individual serving bowls. Serve immediately.

- Wine pairing: Cava
- Start with roasted eggplant soup.

- For dessert, poach pears in red wine and cinnamon sticks; serve with a dollop of sweetened crème fraîche.

IN THE KITCHEN peeling & seeding tomatoes

Peeling and seeding tomatoes is easy if you follow this method.

Bring a small pot of water to a boil over high heat. Prepare an ice-water bath by filling a medium bowl halfway with ice and water. Using the tip of a paring knife, remove the stem, then score the bottom of the tomato with an X. Do the same for all tomatoes you're using in the recipe. Place the tomatoes in the boiling water to completely cover and blanch until the skin just starts to pucker and loosen, about 20 to 30 seconds.

Immediately remove the tomatoes with tongs and immerse them in the ice-water bath. Core the tomatoes and peel the loosened skin; discard the peel and core. Make believe the stem is the North Pole and cut through a tomato across the equator. Cup each tomato half in the palm of your hand and squeeze out the seeds. Dice the tomatoes.

grilled pizza with broccolini, hot peppers & fresh pecorino

1 Tbs. extra-virgin olive oil

2 cloves garlic, minced

6 chopped Calabrian chiles or large pinch crushed red pepper flakes

2 bunches broccolini, coarsely chopped

Kosher salt

1½ cups coarsely grated Italian Fontina (about 5 ounces)

½ cup coarsely grated fresh pecorino (about 3 ounces)

1 recipe Weir Dough (recipe on p. 38)

makes two 11-inch pizzas

SERVING SUGGESTIONS

• Wine pairing: Brunello or Prosecco
• Serve with a fennel, arugula, and radicchio salad with toasted pine nuts and shaved Parmigiano-Reggiano.
• An espresso and biscotti are a perfect ending.

THIS PIZZA DOUGH IS SO DARN GOOD THAT IT DESERVED TO BE named. Gary Danko, my "best chef friend" and renowned San Francisco restaurateur, started calling my dough "Weir Dough" and the name stuck. It has a nice ring to it, doesn't it? Weirdo. I mean, Weir Dough. You won't find a better pizza crust out there. It's perfectly crisp with just a touch of chewiness. The secret is to not work the dough too much when rolling and shaping your pies and to make sure your grill is heated to medium high before sliding the pizza onto the grill. Here I've topped the pizza with a spicy helping of broccolini. Could there be a better way to eat your vegetables? I think not.

1. Heat a grill to medium-high heat.

2. Warm the olive oil in a large frying pan over medium heat. Add the garlic and cook until it softens but doesn't take on any color, 10 to 20 seconds. Immediately add the chiles or pepper flakes, broccolini, and 2 Tbs. water. Toss constantly until the broccolini begins to soften. Season with salt, then set aside and let cool.

3. In a bowl, combine the Fontina and pecorino.

4. Punch down the dough. On a floured surface, divide the dough into 2 round pieces. Roll and form one piece of dough into a 10- to 11-inch circle, ⅜ inch thick, but do not work the dough too much. Transfer to a lightly floured pizza peel, then transfer the pizza onto the grill. Grill until the bottom of the dough is golden, crispy, and firm enough to turn, 2 to 3 minutes. Watch this closely so it doesn't burn.

5. Turn the pizza over and sprinkle half of the combined cheese to within ½ inch of the edge of the dough. Spread half of the broccolini on top of the cheese. Continue to cook until the dough is golden and crispy, about 3 to 4 minutes.

6. Remove the pizza from the grill and cut into wedges. Repeat with the remaining ingredients to make a second pizza.

continued on p. 38

weir dough

2 tsp. active dry yeast

¾ cup plus 1 Tbs. lukewarm water (110°F)

2 cups unbleached bread flour

Kosher salt

In a bowl, combine the yeast, ¼ cup of the lukewarm water, and ¼ cup of the flour. Let it stand for 30 minutes. Add the remaining 1¾ cups flour, ½ cup plus 1 Tbs. warm water, and ½ tsp. salt. Mix the dough thoroughly and turn out onto a floured surface. Knead until smooth, elastic, and a bit tacky to the touch, 7 to 8 minutes. Place in an oiled bowl and turn to cover with oil. Cover with plastic wrap and let rise in a warm place (about 75°F) until it doubles in volume, 1 to 1½ hours. Or, preferably, let the dough rise in the refrigerator overnight. The next day, let it come to room temperature and proceed with the recipe.

making pizza dough

If the dough is proofed correctly, it will bubble up, indicating that the yeast is alive.

Once you learn this technique for making pizza dough, you'll find yourself referring to it time and again.

For proofing the dough, you will need yeast, warm water, and flour. I prefer dry yeast. Make sure you check the yeast to see that it is within the use-by date. And warm water is crucial. It should be 110°F. Let the dough-yeast mixture sit for 20 to 60 minutes until it bubbles up; if it doesn't bubble up, discard and start again.

When kneading the dough, you should work on a lightly floured surface. You'll likely need to add flour as you work the dough, so keep extra handy. With a ball of dough on the surface in front of you, move and stretch the dough, pressing away from you. Fold the dough onto itself to develop a very stretchy dough.

To shape the dough, place it on the back of your slightly closed hands and stretch gently to form a circular shape. It doesn't have to be perfect.

Work the dough while it's in the bowl, kneading it into a ball.

Move and stretch the dough on the work surface, using your thumbs and fingers to stretch it.

After flattening the dough on the work surface, hold it with one hand while laying it across the back of your other hand, pulling gently to stretch it.

sweet corn & spicy jack quesadillas with tomato salsa

3 ears of corn, shucked

1 cup coarsely grated pepper Jack (about 3 ounces)

1 cup coarsely grated white Cheddar (about 3 ounces)

5 green onions, white and green parts, thinly sliced

6 flour tortillas, 8 to 9 inches in diameter

Summer Tomato Salsa, for serving (recipe on the facing page)

serves 6

I'VE EATEN A LOT OF MEXICAN FOOD IN MY DAY. AND I MEAN A LOT. As research for my book *Tequila*, I ate and drank my way through Jalisco and Puerto Vallarta in Mexico. And as I prepared to open my first restaurant, Copita, in Sausalito, California, I tasted every last taco, quesadilla, tamale, and chile relleno I could get my hands on.

What I love about this quesadilla is its simplicity. The zing of oozing pepper Jack and Cheddar cheeses against the sweet snap of the fresh corn can't be beat. Topped with homemade fresh tomato salsa, this quintessential Mexican fare is also a no-fuss dinner.

1. Bring a large saucepan of water to a boil. Add the corn and simmer, turning occasionally, until the kernels turn a slightly darker yellow, 5 to 6 minutes. Remove from the water and let cool. Break each ear of corn in half. Cut the kernels off the cob (see the sidebar on the facing page).

2. Combine the corn kernels, cheeses, and green onions.

3. Place 3 tortillas on a work surface and distribute the mixture evenly over them. Top with the remaining tortillas. Heat a nonstick skillet over medium-high heat and cook the quesadillas, one by one, on one side until light golden, 2 to 3 minutes. Using a large spatula (and with the help the fingers on your other hand), flip the quesadilla and continue to cook on the other side until light golden and the cheese is melted, 2 to 3 minutes.

4. Cut each quesadilla into 6 wedges and serve with salsa.

SERVING SUGGESTIONS

• Drink pairing: Margaritas

• Serve with tortilla chips and guacamole.

• A fun dessert is tres leches ice cream cones.

cutting corn kernels off the cob

To avoid a mess and the corn kernels ending up on the floor, break the corn cobs in half. In a 9 x 13-inch baking dish, hold the cut side of one piece of cob facedown in the pan. Using a sharp knife, cut the kernels off the cob from top to bottom. Rotate the cob as you continue to cut off kernels.

summer tomato salsa

1¼ pounds yellow, orange, and red cherry tomatoes, quartered

⅓ cup chopped fresh cilantro

4 green onions, white and green parts, thinly sliced

5 Tbs. freshly squeezed lime juice

1 whole jalapeño or serrano pepper, seeded and minced

Kosher salt and freshly ground black pepper

makes 3 cups

Place the tomatoes, cilantro, green onions, lime juice, and jalapeño or serrano peppers in a bowl. Mix well and season with salt and pepper.

20-minute baby spinach & gruyère soufflé

5 Tbs. plus 1 tsp. unsalted butter

¼ cup freshly grated Parmigiano-Reggiano

5 Tbs. unbleached all-purpose flour

2 cups half-and-half

Kosher salt and freshly ground black pepper

6 eggs, separated, at room temperature

1½ cups coarsely grated Gruyère

3 cups baby spinach

serves 6

SERVING SUGGESTIONS

• Wine pairing: Sparkling wine

• Serve an arugula salad with lemon-garlic vinaigrette alongside the soufflé.

• End the meal with mint chocolate chip ice cream.

THROUGHOUT THE YEARS OF TEACHING I'VE LEARNED THAT MANY home cooks are intimidated by whipping egg whites to make a soufflé, but there's no need to be. This recipe could not be simpler and is a perfect first soufflé recipe if you've never made one. As long as the eggs whites are properly whipped and gently folded into the soufflé base, success is practically guaranteed. By spooning the soufflé onto a shallow buttered platter, it rises easily and baking time is more than halved. And talk about the "wow" factor—this dish is spectacular!

1. Using 1 tsp. of the butter, grease a 12-inch, oval, ovenproof platter or 4- to 5-quart baking dish. Dust the platter with Parmigiano-Reggiano, tapping out the excess. Alternatively, grease and dust six 1- to 1½-cup ramekins to make individual servings.

2. Melt the remaining 5 Tbs. of butter in a heavy saucepan over medium heat. Add the flour and whisk for a few minutes until the flour is incorporated and no lumps remain. Place the half-and-half in another saucepan over medium-high heat and heat until there are bubbles around the edges of the pan and a skin forms on top (this is called bringing to a scald, when you're heating milk just until boiling). Add the hot cream to the flour and butter mixture, stirring rapidly with a whisk. Cook for a few minutes until the sauce is smooth and thick. Add salt to taste.

3. Add the yolks, one at a time, stirring well after each addition. Let the mixture cool for 10 minutes. Add the Gruyère and season with salt and pepper to taste. Mix well.

4. Heat the oven to 400°F. Place the egg whites in a clean bowl and beat with an electric mixer until stiff peaks form, 5 to 7 minutes. Fold half of the whites into the cheese sauce with as few strokes as possible. Fold in the remaining whites and the baby spinach. Turn the mixture onto the prepared platter or baking dish (or divide among the ramekins if making individual servings).

5. Bake in the top third of the oven until puffed and a skewer inserted into the center is just slightly moist and the top of the soufflé is well browned, 18 to 20 minutes for the platter or baking dish and 18 to 20 minutes for the ramekins. Serve immediately.

IN THE KITCHEN whipping egg whites

For perfectly whipped egg whites without using a mixer, make sure your egg whites are room temperature and place them in a stainless-steel bowl. Place the bowl about 1 to 2 inches above a gas flame or electric burner and swirl the bowl to warm the egg whites slightly. To check, dip you finger into the whites to test whether they are just warm to the touch. Do not let the egg whites turn white and cook.

Using a large balloon whisk, whip the egg whites in a circular motion, incorporating air. Beat until they just begin to hold stiff peaks. You can test this by lifting the whisk out of the egg whites. If it looks as if the whites are blowing in the wind and extended slightly horizontally, they are stiff peaks. If they begin to look grainy, you have gone too far.

spaghetti squash with brown butter & parmesan

2½ to 3 pounds spaghetti squash

⅓ cup pumpkin seeds

3 slices bacon, cut into ½-inch dice

3 Tbs. unsalted butter

¼ tsp. freshly grated nutmeg

3 Tbs. coarsely chopped fresh sage

Kosher salt and freshly ground black pepper

½ cup finely grated Parmigiano-Reggiano

serves 6

SERVING SUGGESTIONS

- Wine pairing: Dry Gewürztraminer
- Serve with carrot and ginger soup.
- Finish the meal with baked apples topped with soft vanilla ice cream.

IF YOU'VE EVER PREPARED SPAGHETTI SQUASH, IT'S QUITE APPARENT how this winter squash got its name. When cooked, its tender flesh separates into delicate strands that very closely resemble spaghetti noodles. In this dish, the "noodles" are then tossed in a sauce of nutty brown butter and sage and topped with crunchy pumpkin seeds and crisp bacon. This meal is especially fitting for anyone avoiding gluten; it is so tasty it's sure to be enjoyed by all.

1. Heat the oven to 375°F.

2. Puncture the squash in 10 places with the tines of a fork. Place the squash on a baking sheet and bake until it can be skewered easily with a knife, about 45 minutes. While the squash is roasting, place the pumpkin seeds on a baking sheet and toast in the oven until golden, 8 to 10 minutes. Remove from the oven and set aside.

3. In the meantime, warm a stainless-steel frying pan over medium-high heat. Add the bacon to the pan and cook, stirring occasionally, until golden and crispy, 3 to 4 minutes. Remove the bacon with a slotted spoon and drain on paper towels.

4. Pour off all but 1 Tbs. of the bacon fat and discard. Add the butter and cook until it bubbles up and gets foamy. Continue to cook the butter until the foam subsides and it begins to turn golden brown and just begins to smoke, 3 to 4 minutes. Remove immediately from the heat and stir in the nutmeg and sage.

4. While the squash is still hot, cut it in half lengthwise and scrape out the seeds with a fork and discard. Using the fork, scrape the remaining squash lengthwise, carefully separating the flesh into spaghetti-like strands and place on a serving plate; sprinkle the strands with salt and pepper as you go. If the butter has cooled, warm it until hot, 30 seconds.

5. To serve, drizzle the butter, pumpkin seeds, and Parmigiano-Reggiano over the top of the squash, distributing evenly. Sprinkle with the bacon and serve immediately.

IN THE KITCHEN making brown butter

To make brown butter, warm butter over medium-high heat in a stainless steel saucepan. After the butter melts, there will be a lot of white foam in the pan on top of the melted butter. As the foam and bubbles subside, watch the butter closely. The particles in the bottom of the pan will turn light golden and then golden as the pan begins to smoke slightly and the butter smells nutty. Immediately remove the pan from the heat.

2

A grain OF TRUTH

THE RECIPES

TECHNIQUES MADE SIMPLE

baked penne with herbed ricotta & summer vegetables

12 ounces penne

Kosher salt and freshly ground pepper

3 medium zucchini (about ¾ pound), cut into ½-inch dice

¾ pound asparagus, cut into 1-inch pieces

¾ cup fresh or frozen English peas

1½ cups whole milk ricotta

1½ cups heavy cream

1 cup finely grated Parmigiano-Reggiano

¼ cup thinly sliced fresh chives

½ cup torn fresh basil leaves

3 Tbs. chopped fresh mint

1 tsp. chopped fresh oregano

2 tsp. freshly grated lemon zest

Olive oil for baking

serves 6

SERVING SUGGESTIONS

- Wine pairing: Pinot Blanc
- For a first course, serve an Italian bread salad with stale bread, lots of summer tomatoes, red onions, cucumbers, and basil.
- For dessert, grill pound cake and top with a berry compote and whipped cream.

THIS DISH STRIKES JUST THE RIGHT BALANCE BETWEEN LIGHT AND refreshing and rich and decadent. The lively lemon zest and herb-studded ricotta and fresh zucchini, asparagus, and peas keep the dish grounded in the bright flavors of summertime, while the creamy cheese mixture and al dente penne provide substance and a hint of indulgence. The combination is quite delicious and incredibly satisfying.

There's no need to stress about the exact herbs or vegetables used in this dish. Use what you have on hand, what is ripe for picking in your garden, or what speaks to you.

1. Heat the oven to 375°F.

2. Bring a large pot of salted water to a boil. Add the pasta and cook until it is al dente, 13 to 16 minutes, or according to the package directions.

3. In the meantime, bring a large saucepan of salted water to a boil over high heat. Add the zucchini and asparagus and cook, uncovered, until the vegetables are almost tender, 3 minutes. Add the peas and continue to cook for 1 minute. Remove the vegetables from the pan with a slotted spoon and place in a bowl.

4. When the pasta is al dente, drain and set aside.

5. In a separate bowl, combine the ricotta cheese, heavy cream, half of the Parmigiano-Reggiano, the chives, basil, mint, oregano, and lemon zest. Stir together until well combined. Season with salt and pepper.

6. Combine the pasta, ricotta mixture, and vegetables in a large bowl. Season with salt and pepper and place in an oiled, 9 x 9-inch, baking dish. Sprinkle with the remaining Parmigiano-Reggiano. Cover loosely with foil and bake on the top rack of the oven for 10 minutes. Remove the foil and continue to cook until the cheese is bubbling and the top is light golden, 10 to 15 minutes. Serve immediately.

wild and brown rice with mushrooms & chard

½ ounce dried porcini mushrooms

4 cups low-sodium chicken stock

Kosher salt and freshly ground black pepper

1 cup wild rice

1 cup brown rice

2 Tbs. extra-virgin olive oil

1 small yellow onion, minced

1 stalk celery, cut into ¼-inch dice

2 cloves garlic, minced

1 pound fresh button mushrooms, sliced

1 bunch Swiss chard, stems removed and discarded, cut into 1-inch pieces

2 Tbs. chopped fresh flat-leaf parsley

2 tsp. chopped fresh sage

1 tsp. chopped fresh thyme

serves 6

SERVING SUGGESTIONS

- Wine pairing: Sangiovese
- Start with roasted cauliflower soup.
- For dessert, serve pineapple chunks drizzled with extra-virgin olive oil and sprinkled with fleur de sel.

YOU MAY BE SURPRISED BY HOW MEATY AND FLAVORFUL THIS RICE bowl is despite the absence of any real meat (other than chicken stock, which could be replaced with vegetable stock for a vegetarian dish). Mushrooms are to thank for that incredible depth of flavor. The residual liquid from reconstituting the dried porcinis provides a wallop of umami, which permeates the rice as it cooks. The button mushrooms, sautéed with herbs and vitamin-rich Swiss chard, contribute amazing meaty texture. Even the fiercest meat-eaters will not be left wanting with this dish. While it's hearty enough to serve as a main course, it's also wonderful as a side.

1. Pour 1 cup boiling water over the dried mushrooms and let sit until the water is cool. Strain the mushrooms, reserving the liquid. Chop the mushrooms coarsely. If the mushrooms are sandy, strain the mushroom liquid through a paper towel or cheesecloth-lined fine-mesh strainer.

2. Place the mushroom liquid in a large saucepan. Add the chicken stock and 1 tsp. salt and bring to a boil over high heat. Reduce the heat to low, add the wild rice, cover, and simmer slowly for 15 minutes. Add the brown rice, stir, cover, and simmer until all the rice is tender and the liquid has been absorbed, 40 to 45 minutes.

3. In the meantime, warm the oil in a large frying pan over medium-high heat. Add the onions and celery and cook until the vegetables are soft, 10 minutes. Add the garlic and fresh and reconstituted dry mushrooms and cook, stirring occasionally, for 2 to 3 minutes.

4. Add the Swiss chard to the mushrooms and cook until the chard is almost tender but still bright green, 3 to 4 minutes. Season with salt and pepper.

5. When the rice is done, remove the cover and add the mushroom-chard mixture, the parsley, sage, and thyme. Toss together and season to taste with salt and pepper. Serve immediately.

bulgur, feta & oven-dried tomato salad

1 cup medium-fine bulgur or cracked wheat

½ cup extra-virgin olive oil

5 cloves garlic, minced

¾ cup freshly squeezed lemon juice; more as needed

1 large bunch green onions, white and green parts, diced

1 cup chopped fresh flat-leaf parsley

½ cup chopped fresh mint

1 recipe Oven-Dried Tomatoes (recipe on the facing page)

1 large English cucumber, peeled, seeded, and diced

Kosher salt and freshly ground black pepper

6 ounces barrel-aged feta

serves 6

SERVING SUGGESTIONS

• Wine pairing: Dry rosé

• Serve this salad accompanied by warm pita bread, romaine leaves that you can use like a spoon, and a bowl of hummus.

I ORIGINALLY MADE THIS SALAD AS A SIDE DISH TO SERVE AT A dinner party I was hosting, and it absolutely stole the show. I now let it take center stage as a healthy, hearty Mediterranean-inspired main course salad. Made with bulgur, a fiber- and protein-rich form of whole wheat that has been precooked, the preparation is quite simple but does require some advanced planning, as it benefits from 24 to 48 hours of refrigeration. The oven-dried tomatoes are also very easy to make but require 5 to 6 hours in the oven. Trust me, this salad is worth the wait and is the perfect make-ahead dish.

Slow-roasting the tomatoes brings out their natural sweetness, which combines perfectly with the nutty bulgur, salty feta, and citrusy vinaigrette.

1. Place the bulgur on the bottom of a large salad bowl. In a small bowl, whisk together the olive oil, garlic, and lemon juice and drizzle over the bulgur. Layer the green onions, parsley, mint, tomatoes, and cucumbers, in that order, on top of the bulgur. Season the top layer with 2 tsp. salt and ¼ tsp. pepper. Crumble the feta on the top. Cover with plastic wrap and refrigerate for at least 24 hours and up to 48 hours.

2. Bring the salad to room temperature. Taste and season with 1 tsp. salt and more lemon juice if needed. Serve with romaine leaves or warm pita bread.

oven-dried tomatoes

2 pounds plum tomatoes, cored
and cut in half lengthwise

1 Tbs. kosher salt

makes 1½ cups

1. Place the tomatoes, cut side up, on a baking sheet and sprinkle with the
salt. Let sit for 1 hour.

2. Heat the oven to 250°F.

3. Bake the tomatoes until they are almost dry, yet still slightly soft and
plump, 5 to 6 hours.

cheesy spaghetti pie

5 large eggs, lightly beaten

1 cup finely grated Parmigiano-Reggiano or Grana Padano

½ cup finely grated pecorino

2 tsp. chopped fresh oregano

Kosher salt and freshly ground black pepper

4 ounces Gorgonzola, crumbled

4 cups cooked or leftover spaghetti

1 Tbs. unsalted butter

serves 6

SERVING SUGGESTIONS

- Drink pairing: As an aperitif, serve spritzers made with 1 Tbs. Aperol® topped with ice cold Prosecco.
- As a side dish, serve grilled radicchio halves, drizzled with a balsamic and shallot vinaigrette.

I ALWAYS HAVE LEFTOVER PASTA AND A MILLION TINY NUGGETS of every cheese imaginable in the fridge. In an attempt to use up various leftovers I came up with this recipe, which is so delicious and soul warming; it's the ultimate comfort food. Prepared just like a frittata, spaghetti is bound with eggs and cooked in a frying pan, producing a crisp and golden crust. When the spaghetti pie is sliced, the interior is nicely dense and incredibly creamy, oozing with Parmigiano-Reggiano, pecorino, and bold Gorgonzola. You're going to love this one!

1. Place the eggs in a large bowl and whisk until light and frothy. Add the Parmigiano-Reggiano, pecorino, oregano, 1 tsp. salt, and a large pinch of pepper. Add the Gorgonzola along with the spaghetti. Stir the mixture together until well combined.

2. Melt the butter in a 10-inch, nonstick frying pan over medium heat. Add the spaghetti mixture and flatten to cover the bottom of the pan evenly. Cook, uncovered, until the bottom is set and light golden brown, 9 to 10 minutes.

3. Slide the pie out of the pan and onto a large flat plate. Invert the pan over the pie and flip the pan and plate over. Now the pie will be back in the pan with the golden side on top. Continue to cook the pie on the second side until the bottom is set and light golden brown, 9 to 10 minutes. Let cool for 2 minutes, then cut into wedges and serve.

IN THE PANTRY storing cheese

It's always good to have a nice big chunk of Parmigiano-Reggiano in your refrigerator. I like to store it wrapped in a paper towel and then wrapped in plastic wrap. Stored this way in a dry part of your refrigerator (in my case that's a drawer), it will keep for at least 2 months. You can do the same with other grating cheeses like Grana Padano or pecorino. You can also buy these cheeses already grated, but avoid the one that's in a sealed jar—you want to look for freshly grated Parmigiano-Reggiano. While pregrated isn't quite as flavorful as your own, it's a pretty good substitute. To grate a chunk yourself, use a box grater or put the cheese in your food processor.

farro risotto with red wine & grana padano

1 cup chicken stock

2 Tbs. extra-virgin olive oil

1 small yellow onion, finely chopped

2 cups farro (10 ounces)

2¼ cups fruity red wine, such as Grenache or Merlot

Kosher salt and freshly ground black pepper

1 Tbs. unsalted butter

¼ tsp. ground nutmeg

¾ cup freshly grated Grana Padano or Parmigiano-Reggiano

serves 6

THIS RISOTTO IS QUITE UNIQUE, MADE WITH FARRO IN PLACE OF traditional Italian short-grain rice, but the preparation remains the same. It's an ideal cooking technique to master because there are endless variations on risotto. You just have to remember to "toast" the grain before you begin adding liquid and then be patient, stirring constantly and allowing each batch of liquid to be absorbed before adding another. There's something very soothing about the entire process. Wait until you taste (and see!) this version—it's rich, creamy, and a stunning vibrant red.

Using farro, an ancient whole grain from the wheat family, makes this dish a great choice for the health conscious.

1. In a saucepan, combine the chicken stock and 1 cup water and bring to a boil over high heat. Reduce the heat to low and maintain just below the boiling point on a back burner of the stove. Place a ladle in the stock.

2. In a large heavy saucepan over medium heat, warm the olive oil. Add the onions and cook, stirring occasionally, until soft, about 10 minutes. Add the farro and cook, stirring to coat with the oil, and "toast" the farro, 2 minutes. Add ¼ cup of the wine and cook, stirring until it is absorbed, about 1 minute.

3. Add ¼ tsp. of salt and a ladle of stock and stir the farro constantly to wipe it away from the bottom and sides of the pot. When most of the liquid has been absorbed but the farro is still loose, add another ladleful of stock and continue to cook the risotto. Continue to add stock a ladleful at a time, stirring constantly, until the stock is gone. In the empty stock saucepan, add the remaining 2 cups red wine and heat over medium heat. When the farro has absorbed all the stock, add the red wine, a ladleful at a time, until the farro is tender, about 25 to 30 minutes total. If you run out of wine and the farro isn't tender yet and needs additional cooking time, add hot water.

- Wine pairing: Grenache
- For a first course, serve a roasted carrot soup swirled with a dollop of mascarpone and topped with a few crispy croutons.
- For dessert, serve shortbread cookies and caramel ice cream sprinkled with a light dusting of Maldon salt.

4. Remove the pan from the stove and stir in another ladleful of red wine or hot water, the butter, nutmeg, and half of the Grana Padano or Parmigiano. Season to taste with salt and pepper. Cover and let sit off the heat for 5 minutes.

5. Remove the cover, stir, and serve immediately, sprinkled with the remaining cheese.

IN THE PANTRY farro

Farro is an ancient wheat grain that comes from the Mediterranean. It resembles brown rice and has a nutty taste. When cooked, it has a chewy texture that makes it a perfect addition to soups, salads, and risotto. Often called spelt in the United States, farro is a mainstay in Tuscany and other regions of Italy but is fast becoming popular in the United States as well.

fregola, clams & tomatoes

3 pounds fresh Manila clams, scrubbed and rinsed well

¼ cup extra-virgin olive oil

3 cloves garlic, minced

2 cups fregola (about 16 ounces)

2 tomatoes, peeled, seeded, and chopped (fresh or canned)

Pinch of crushed red pepper flakes

3 Tbs. chopped fresh flat-leaf parsley

3 cups chicken stock

Kosher salt and freshly ground black pepper

serves 6

SERVING SUGGESTIONS

• Wine pairing: Greco or Fiano

• As a first course, make a tomato soup flavored with orange.

• For dessert, serve strawberries and raspberries drizzled with aged balsamic vinegar.

FREGOLA IS A TYPE OF PASTA THAT'S SHAPED LIKE SMALL BEADS AND could be mistaken for Israeli couscous. Rather than boiling the pasta in salted water, fregola is prepared in a manner similar to rice. Here, it is "toasted" with olive oil and garlic, then simmered with diced tomatoes, chicken stock, and clam juice. The resulting pasta has a texture and flavor similar to couscous. If you can't find fregola, Israeli couscous is a good substitute.

1. Place the clams and 2 Tbs. of water in a large frying pan over medium-high heat. Cover the pan and cook until the shells open, 4 to 5 minutes. Remove the clams with a slotted spoon and place in a bowl (discard any that don't open). Let the clams cool for 5 minutes. Shuck all but 10 clams and reserve in a separate bowl; discard the shells. Set aside the 10 clams, and reserve the steaming liquid.

2. In a large frying pan over medium heat, warm the oil and add the garlic. Cook, stirring often, until the garlic is light golden, 1 minute. Add the fregola to the pan and stir to coat the grains well with the oil, 1 minute. Add the tomatoes, red pepper flakes, 2 Tbs. of the parsley, the chicken stock, and the reserved clam juice and stir together. Simmer uncovered until the fregola is double in size and firm to the bite but cooked through, 20 to 25 minutes.

3. Just before serving, add the shucked clams and stir together. Season with salt and pepper. Transfer the fregola to a deep serving platter. Garnish with the reserved clams in their shells and sprinkle the remaining 1 Tbs. parsley on top. Serve immediately.

IN THE PANTRY fregola

Fregola, or Sardinian pasta, is similar to Israeli couscous. To make it, semolina dough is rolled into tiny balls and toasted in the oven, hence the golden color and nutty flavor. Made of wheat, it's simple to cook and has a delicate texture. You can find it in Italian markets or well-stocked grocery stores. Uncooked fregola will keep, tightly sealed, in a dry place for at least 6 months.

lamb, barley & white bean stew

¾ cup dry white navy beans
(about 5 ounces)

1½ pounds lamb stew meat, cut
from the leg, cut into 1-inch pieces,
trimmed

2 Tbs. unbleached all-purpose flour

Kosher salt and freshly ground
black pepper

3 Tbs. extra-virgin olive oil

½ tsp. chopped fresh rosemary

½ tsp. chopped fresh thyme

2 bay leaves

3 cloves garlic, minced

6 cups beef stock

6 medium carrots, cut into
1½-inch lengths

18 pearl onions, peeled

¼ cup pearl barley

1 pound medium-size red potatoes,
quartered

1 cup shelled English peas (fresh
or frozen)

Fresh, flat-leaf parsley leaves
for garnish

serves 6

THIS ONE-POT WONDER IS NOT JUST EASY TO PREPARE, BUT IT'S
also hearty and healthy. The combination of tender white navy
beans, chewy pearled barley, and waxy red potatoes gives this stew
fantastic body and texture while the herbs complement the lamb but
allow it to truly shine. Throw in some vegetables and this meal is a
real winner. Even better, there's only one pot to clean!

This is a fantastic make-ahead dish. It can be made up to
2 days in advance and stored in the refrigerator until ready to serve.
Just before serving, warm the stew over medium heat, stirring
occasionally, until bubbling, 5 to 10 minutes.

1. Pick over the beans and discard any stones. Cover with plenty of water
and soak overnight at room temperature. Drain.

2. Place the lamb pieces, flour, ½ teaspoon salt, and ¼ teaspoon black
pepper in a zip-top plastic bag and shake to coat the lamb with flour.
Warm the oil in a large, heavy, soup pot over medium-high heat and cook
the meat in a single layer with space in between until golden brown on
all sides, 10 minutes. You may have to do this in two batches; if so, add
a bit more oil if needed for the second batch. Add the rosemary, thyme,
bay leaves, garlic, the drained white beans, and the stock. Bring to a boil,
reduce the heat to low, and simmer, covered, for 1 hour.

3. Add the carrots, onions, and barley and simmer, uncovered, for
30 minutes. Add the potatoes and simmer, uncovered, for 30 minutes.
Add the peas and simmer, uncovered, for 5 minutes. Season with salt
and pepper.

4. Ladle into bowls and serve immediately garnished with parsley.

SERVING SUGGESTIONS

- Wine pairing: Dolcetto
- As an appetizer, serve dates stuffed
with goat cheese.

- Alongside the stew, serve grilled
bread that's been rubbed with a garlic
clove, brushed with extra-virgin olive
oil, and sprinkled with kosher salt.

orecchiette with cauliflower, brown butter & fried capers

1 head cauliflower (about 2 pounds), cut into florets with ½ inch of the stem removed

6 Tbs. extra-virgin olive oil

Kosher salt and freshly ground black pepper

4 Tbs. unsalted butter

3 cloves garlic, minced

Large pinch of crushed red pepper flakes

12 ounces dry orecchiette

¼ cup capers, rinsed and patted dry

2 tsp. freshly grated lemon zest

1 cup grated Parmigiano-Reggiano

serves 6

SERVING SUGGESTIONS

• Wine pairing: Dry Riesling

• Before dinner, place a chunk of feta cheese in the center of a plate. Surround it with roasted peppers, cured artichoke hearts, and a variety of olives. Drizzle the feta with extra-virgin olive oil and a sprinkling of chopped fresh oregano. Serve with a sliced baguette.

• For dessert, caramelize pears with brown sugar, raisins, and dark rum and top with a dollop of plain Greek yogurt.

IF YOU'VE NEVER ROASTED CAULIFLOWER IN THE OVEN, I ENCOURAGE you to try it. The heat from the oven caramelizes the sugar in the vegetable, bringing out its natural sweetness. And the texture is absolutely perfect: just tender with a crisp bite. In this pasta dish, that sweetness is balanced with heat from red pepper flakes and salt from briny fried capers. Brown butter sauce binds all of the flavors together.

1. Heat the oven to 400°F.

2. Place the cauliflower in a 9 x 13-inch baking pan and toss with 3 Tbs. of the oil. Season with salt and pepper. Roast the cauliflower in the upper third of the oven until light golden and tender, about 30 to 40 minutes.

3. In a large frying pan, melt the butter and cook until the foam subsides and the milk solids turn golden brown and just begin to smoke. Remove the pan from the heat and add the garlic, cauliflower, and red pepper flakes. Toss together.

4. Bring a pot of water to a boil, add the orecchiette, and cook until al dente, 12 to 14 minutes, or according to the package directions.

5. In the meantime, warm the remaining 3 Tbs. oil in a small frying pan over medium-high heat until the oil ripples. Add the capers and cook until crispy and golden, about 1 minute. Drain on paper towels.

6. When the orecchiette is done, drain it and toss with the cauliflower, capers, and lemon zest. Season with salt. Place in a serving bowl and garnish with the Parmigiano. Serve immediately.

grain-filled summer bell peppers

2 Tbs. olive oil

6 green onions, white and green parts, thinly sliced

2 cloves garlic, minced

²⁄₃ cup basmati or jasmine rice

Kosher salt and freshly ground black pepper

4 cups chicken stock

3 Tbs. tomato paste

½ cup amaranth

½ cup quinoa

½ cup millet

6 medium bell peppers (yellow, orange, green, and/or red)

1¼ cups grated Fontina (about 5 ounces)

serves 6

IT'S HARD TO IGNORE ALL THE BUZZ REGARDING THE HEALTH BENEFITS of ancient whole grains. And why would you? Amaranth and quinoa are touted as "super foods" that supply many important nutrients, including fiber, iron, calcium, and protein. If you think incorporating these grains into your diet means eating food that tastes like cardboard, think again!

Here, a beautifully seasoned four-grain pilaf is prepared with long-grain rice, amaranth, quinoa, and millet, then mixed with creamy Italian fontina. The grain mixture is then stuffed into vibrant, steamed bell peppers and baked in the oven until the peppers are just tender. The result is a stunning dish that satisfies both body and soul.

1. Heat the oil in a large saucepan over medium heat. Add the onions and cook, stirring, until soft, 3 minutes. Add the garlic and continue to cook, stirring, until aromatic, about 1 minute.

2. Add the rice and stir to coat with the oil, 1 minute. Add 1 tsp. salt, pepper to taste, 2 cups of the chicken stock, 1½ cups of water, and the tomato paste. Stir well to dissolve the tomato paste. Bring to a boil, reduce the heat to low, and simmer, covered, for 10 minutes. Add the amaranth, quinoa, and millet and stir. Simmer, covered, until the grains are tender and the liquid is absorbed, 15 minutes. Season to taste with salt and pepper. Let cool.

3. Heat the oven to 375°F.

4. Remove the tops from the peppers by slicing ¼ inch of the top off; reserve the tops. Using the tip of a paring knife, carefully remove the seeds and membranes from the peppers, leaving the shell of the pepper intact. Place the remaining 2 cups of the stock in the bottom of a pan or in a steamer and place the peppers in one layer standing upright. Steam the peppers until they begin to soften, 7 to 10 minutes. Reserve the stock.

continued on p. 62

- Wine pairing: Light Pinot Noir
- Start with a fennel, parsley, and radicchio salad tossed with an orange vinaigrette.
- Have a chocolate tasting for dessert.

5. Add the cheese to the cooled grain mixture. Fill the peppers with the grain mixture, distributing it evenly. Pack the peppers into a baking dish close together. Place the tops of the peppers back onto the top of each respective pepper. Pour the reserved stock into the bottom of the dish. Cover loosely with foil and bake for 20 minutes. Remove the foil and continue to bake until the peppers are almost soft, 20 to 25 minutes.

6. To serve, remove the peppers and place one on each plate.

IN THE PANTRY storing grains

Whole grains can be purchased, often in bulk, at most grocery stores or ordered online from various vendors, including Bob's Red Mill®. Other grains that I like to have on hand are polenta, barley, oats, farro, and a number of rices: basmati, jasmine, brown, and risotto. All of these pantry staples can be stored, tightly sealed, at room temperature for up to 6 months

warm orzo, chicken & citrus pilaf

1 orange

1 lemon

Kosher salt

3 chicken breasts (about 6 to 8 ounces each), skinned and boned

2 cups orzo

2 Tbs. extra-virgin olive oil

½ cup dried apricots, cut into ½-inch dice

½ cup dried cranberries, cut into ½-inch dice

¼ cup dried apples, cut into ½-inch dice

¼ cup dried figs, cut into ½-inch dice

1 Tbs. chopped fresh flat-leaf parsley

Freshly ground black pepper

serves 6

EVERY OUNCE OF FLAVOR FROM THE LEMON AND ORANGE COMES through in this recipe, including the peel, zest, and juice. The combination gives the orzo an intense sweet-and-sour punch and makes a dish that's refreshing and vibrant.

1. With a paring knife, remove one 2-inch-long strip from both the orange and the lemon. With a knife, scrape away any white pith from the back of the peel. Set aside.

2. Finely zest 2 tsp. of the orange and 2 tsp. of the lemon. Combine and set aside.

3. Bring a large saucepan of salted water to a boil. Add the chicken breasts and simmer until firm to the touch and cooked through, 10 to 12 minutes. Transfer to a plate and cover loosely with foil.

4. Bring a pot of salted water to a boil. Add the lemon and orange peel and the orzo and simmer until the orzo is done, 7 to 9 minutes. In the meantime, shred the chicken into ½-inch strips. Cover with foil and set aside.

5. Cut the orange and lemon in half and squeeze 1 Tbs. of the juice from each into a small bowl.

6. When the orzo is done, drain and discard the peel. Add the oil, orange and lemon juice, orange and lemon zest, chicken, dried fruit, and parsley. Toss together and season to taste with salt and pepper. Serve immediately.

SERVING SUGGESTIONS

- Wine pairing: Viognier or Torrontés

- A mixed green salad with shaved fennel is a great side dish along with crusty wheat rolls.

orecchiette with lemon chicken & herb salad

⅓ cup plus 1 Tbs. extra-virgin olive oil

3 Tbs. freshly squeezed lemon juice

2 cloves garlic, minced

1 tsp. ground cumin

Kosher salt and freshly ground black pepper

3 boneless, skinless chicken breasts (about 1 pound)

4 cups chicken stock

1 pound 100% semolina dry orecchiette

1½ cups fresh arugula

¾ cup fresh cilantro sprigs

¾ cup fresh basil leaves, torn into large pieces

½ cup fresh mint leaves

½ cup fresh flat-leaf parsley leaves

1 preserved lemon, peel only, cut into ¼-inch dice

serves 6

ORECCHIETTE MEANS "LITTLE EARS" IN ITALIAN, AND IN THIS
delicious dish the whimsical pasta is combined with tender, moist, grilled chicken. The sauce is bright, fresh, and rich all at the same time. A salad of fresh herbs wilts gently into the bed of pasta and adds depth, while the preserved lemon peel adds mild tartness and bursts of intense lemon flavor. My cooking assistant, Bruce Fielding, tells everyone that this is his favorite recipe ever. Thanks, Bruce!

1. If you are cooking indoors, heat a cast-iron, ridged grill pan over medium heat for 10 minutes. Otherwise, start a charcoal or gas grill.

2. In a large bowl, whisk together ⅓ cup of oil, the lemon juice, garlic, cumin, and salt and pepper to taste. Reserve.

3. Brush the chicken breasts with the remaining 1 Tbs. of oil. Cook the chicken until golden on one side, 3 to 4 minutes. Turn the chicken over, season with salt and pepper, and continue to cook until done, 4 to 5 minutes. Place the chicken on a work surface and cover with an inverted bowl; let cool for 5 minutes. With your fingers, tear the chicken with the grain into thin pieces. Reserve.

4. Place the chicken stock in a saucepan over high heat and cook until it's reduced to 1 cup. Add the oil and lemon juice mixture and set aside.

5. Bring a large pot of salted water to a boil. Add the orecchiette and cook until al dente, 10 to 12 minutes, or according to the package directions. Drain the pasta and put back in the pot; immediately add the stock, chicken, arugula, cilantro, basil, mint, parsley, preserved lemons, and salt and pepper to taste. Toss well, place on a platter, and serve immediately.

continued on p. 66

- Wine pairing: Un-oaked Chardonnay or Arneis

- To start, serve an asparagus soup drizzled with crème fraîche.

- For dessert, serve a cheese plate garnished with toasted pecans, toasted almonds, dried figs, and dried apricots.

IN THE KITCHEN creating a steam tent

Bowls come in handy in the kitchen for more than just tossing a salad or making chocolate chip cookies. I like to invert a bowl over roasted peppers when they have been just charred; this creates steam under the bowl that separates the skin from the pepper away from the flesh of the pepper. I use the same principle for the chicken in this recipe. By inverting a bowl over the chicken, a steam tent is created, keeping the chicken moist. You will see how juicy it is when you tear the chicken into pieces.

piadine with arugula & plum salad

2 Tbs. balsamic vinegar

2 Tbs. extra-virgin olive oil; more for the dough

1 shallot, minced

Kosher salt and freshly ground black pepper

1 recipe Weir Dough (recipe on p. 68)

Unbleached all-purpose flour

6 cups loosely packed arugula

2 plums, halved, pitted, and thinly sliced

½ cup roasted and salted pistachios

makes 2 piadine, 12 to 13 inches in diameter; serves 6

SERVING SUGGESTIONS

• Wine pairing: Pinot Grigio

• Combine warm mixed olives with rosemary, fennel seed, crushed red pepper flakes, and olive oil; serve with baguette slices.

• For dessert, serve lemon sorbet drizzled with Limoncello.

IF YOU'RE ANYTHING LIKE ME, YOU ALWAYS ORDER A SALAD WITH your favorite pizza when eating out. This dinner joins pizza and a salad in my version of Italy's *piadine insalata*, a thin flatbread topped with a salad, traditionally made in the Emilia Romagna. Here, I've taken my recipe for the perfect pizza dough and topped it with peppery arugula, juicy plums, and crunchy pistachios. It's the best of both worlds.

1. Heat the oven to 550°F.

2. In a small bowl, whisk together the vinegar, oil, and shallot. Season with salt and pepper.

3. Punch down the dough. On a floured surface, divide the dough into two pieces and form each into a round ball. Stretch one ball of dough into a 12- to 13-inch circle, ¼ to ⅛ inch thick. If it is difficult for you to shape the dough this large, let the dough rest for 5 minutes and try again. If needed, use a rolling pin to facilitate the shaping process.

4. Transfer the circle of dough to a well-floured pizza stone or peel. Lightly brush the dough to within ½ inch of the edge with oil. Using the sharp tines of a fork, puncture the dough several times (this will prevent it from forming big bubbles in the oven). Slide the pizza onto the pizza stone and bake until golden and crisp, 8 to 10 minutes. In the meantime, toss half of the arugula, plums, and pistachios with the half of the vinaigrette.

5. Remove the pizza and top with the salad and serve immediately. (Don't wait to serve this until the second pizza is ready. The pizza should be served hot because the texture changes as the pizza cools.)

6. Continue with the remaining ingredients to make a second piadine.

continued on p. 68

weir dough

2 tsp. active dry yeast

¾ cup plus 1 Tbs. lukewarm water (110°F)

2 cups unbleached bread flour

Kosher salt

In a bowl, combine the yeast, ¼ cup of the lukewarm water, and ¼ cup of the flour. Let stand for 30 minutes. Add the remaining 1¾ cups flour, ½ cup plus 1 Tbs. warm water, and ½ tsp. salt. Mix the dough thoroughly and turn out onto a floured surface. Knead until smooth, elastic, and a bit tacky to the touch, 7 to 8 minutes. Place in an oiled bowl and turn to cover with oil. Cover with plastic wrap and let rise in a warm place (about 75°F) until it doubles in volume, 1 to 1½ hours. Or, preferably, let the dough rise in the refrigerator overnight. The next day, let it come to room temperature and proceed with the recipe.

polenta & goat cheese soufflé

1 Tbs. unsalted butter

5 Tbs. plus ⅓ cup grated Parmigiano-Reggiano

3 cups milk

¾ cup polenta

½ tsp. chopped fresh rosemary

4 large egg yolks

5 ounces fresh goat cheese

Kosher salt and freshly ground pepper

5 large egg whites, at room temperature

serves 6

EVERYONE'S FEAR ABOUT SOUFFLÉS IS WHIPPING THE EGG WHITES.
Make sure when you separate the whites from the yolks that you don't have any yolk in with the white; egg whites won't whip in the presence of fat. It's also best to have your egg whites at room temperature. Use a big balloon whisk or even hold two whisks in one hand and whisk vigorously. The more spokes or prongs you have on the whisk, the faster your egg whites will whip.

This is not your standard egg soufflé. The addition of creamy polenta to the soufflé base makes for a firmer-textured, more substantial version of the classic French dish. A single bite is sure to bring a smile to your face.

1. Using 1 Tbs. of the butter, grease six individual soufflé dishes or ramekins (1¼ to 1½ cups each) and dust with 3 Tbs. of the Parmigiano-Reggiano, tapping out the excess. Set aside.

2. Bring the milk to a scald over medium heat, watching carefully so it doesn't boil over. Add the polenta and rosemary in a slow, steady stream, whisking constantly. Cook the polenta, stirring constantly, until it is the consistency of a thick white sauce, about 5 to 10 minutes. Remove from the heat and let cool for 10 minutes.

3. Using a wooden spoon, add the egg yolks to the polenta mixture one at a time, beating well after each addition. Crumble the goat cheese into the mixture, add ⅓ cup of the Parmigiano-Reggiano, and beat until it is well mixed. Season with salt and pepper. The soufflé can be prepared in advance up to this point. If you won't be finishing the soufflé for several hours, set the base in the refrigerator. If you are using it within the hour, you can leave it at room temperature.

- Wine pairing: Sauvignon Blanc
- The perfect accompaniment for this soufflé is a fresh cauliflower, diced red onion, and olive salad tossed with your favorite dressing.
- For dessert, serve chocolate truffles and hot mocha drinks.

4. About 1 hour before serving, heat the oven to 375°F.

5. Place the egg whites in a large bowl and whip by hand or use an electric mixer to beat the egg whites until they hold a firm peak. Fold a quarter of the egg whites into the polenta mixture, then fold in the remaining egg whites. Spoon the mixture into the prepared soufflé dishes, distributing evenly. Sprinkle the tops with the remaining 2 Tbs. of the Parmigiano-Reggiano.

6. Place the filled soufflé dishes on a baking sheet with space in between each one. Bake the soufflés until well puffed, golden brown, and almost firm, 30 to 40 minutes. Serve immediately.

IN THE KITCHEN scalding milk

There are many cooking terms that we cooks take for granted. Scalding is one of them. To scald milk, place the milk in a saucepan. Turn the heat to medium high and don't walk away. Don't stir either. What you are looking for is bubbles around the edges and a skin that forms on the top. As soon as that happens, remove the pan from the heat. Boiled milk, unlike boiled water, has a tendency to boil over the edges of the pan so watch closely.

soft polenta with sausages, tomatoes & peppers

Kosher salt and freshly ground black pepper

2½ cups polenta

3 Tbs. extra-virgin olive oil

1 medium yellow onion, minced

2 yellow bell peppers, seeded and cut into ½-inch slices

6 links hot Italian pork sausage (about 2 pounds)

3 cups peeled, seeded, and chopped tomatoes (fresh or canned)

3 Tbs. unsalted butter

1 tsp. chopped fresh rosemary

1 cup grated Parmigiano-Reggiano

serves 6

THIS CASUAL ITALIAN DISH MAKES A WONDERFUL WEEKNIGHT MEAL. Polenta, made with yellow or white cornmeal, is a gluten-free alternative to pasta—and almost as easy to make. Its texture is smooth and creamy, even when prepared with just water.

Topped with sautéed, sweet bell peppers and spicy, hot pork sausage, this polenta dish is a palate pleaser. Just don't forget to taste and season the polenta with salt before serving; otherwise, it may fall flat. Keep in mind that the Parmigiano-Reggiano garnish will add another touch of saltiness.

1. Bring 8 cups of water to a boil in a large saucepan over high heat. Add 1½ tsp. salt. In a slow, steady stream, add the polenta, whisking constantly. As soon as the polenta has been added and it begins to thicken, reduce the heat to low and change to a wooden spoon. Stir the polenta occasionally until it's thick and a spoon can stand up in it, 30 minutes.

2. In the meantime, warm the oil in a large frying pan over medium heat. Add the onions and peppers and cook, stirring occasionally, until soft, 10 minutes. Prick the sausages all over a few times with a fork. Add the sausages to the frying pan and cook, uncovered, until they are firm, 12 to 15 minutes. Remove the sausages from the pan and cut each one into two pieces on the diagonal. Return the sausages to the pan.

3. Add the tomatoes, increase the heat to medium high, and simmer, uncovered, until the tomatoes thicken, 10 minutes. Season with salt and pepper.

4. When the polenta is done, stir in the butter, rosemary, and salt and pepper to taste. To serve, spoon the polenta on a serving plate, make a well in the center, and carefully pour the sausages and tomato sauce into the well. Garnish with Parmigiano-Reggiano and serve immediately.

- Wine pairing: Barbera or Chianti

- For a first course, serve crostini topped with herb-scented goat cheese and wilted baby spinach.

- For dessert, chill glasses of Moscato and serve with a halved strawberry in each glass.

IN THE KITCHEN cooking polenta

Polenta is so easy to make at home, but to ensure it doesn't get lumpy as it cooks, here are a few tips: When adding the polenta to the water, do so in a slow, steady stream, whisking constantly. Continue to whisk until you feel a texture change—the polenta will start to thicken. At that point, change from a whisk to a wooden spoon and reduce the heat (if the heat is too high, the polenta can pop and spatter and you can easily burn yourself). Continue to stir periodically until a spoon almost stands in the polenta.

For added flavor, you can add rosemary and lots of grated Parmigiano-Reggiano. And don't be afraid of adding salt. Polenta cries out for it.

quick risotto with shrimp & meyer lemon

4 Tbs. extra-virgin olive oil

1½ pounds medium shrimp
(36 to 40 per pound), peeled and
deveined

1 cup dry white wine, such as
Sauvignon Blanc or Pinot Grigio

2 cups bottled clam juice or
fish stock

1 medium yellow onion, finely diced

2 cups arborio, vialone nano, or
carnaroli rice

1 Meyer lemon

2 Tbs. unsalted butter

¾ cup grated Parmigiano-
Reggiano

Kosher salt and freshly ground
black pepper

Fresh flat-leaf parsley leaves,
for garnish

serves 6

THE TRADITIONAL METHOD FOR PREPARING RISOTTO REQUIRES YOU
to stand over the pan, stirring constantly. While I actually find the
process quite enjoyable and somehow relaxing, I realize that it
doesn't make for a simple supper. That's why I came up with this
no-fuss method. My trick? After the risotto simmers on its own for
20 minutes without stirring, I remove it from the heat, add an extra
ladleful of hot water, and allow it to sit for 5 minutes. This easy process
produces risotto that is deliciously creamy with perfect texture.

In this recipe, Meyer lemon, a cross between a true lemon and a
mandarin orange, serves as the perfect slightly sweet complement
to the sautéed shrimp. If you can't find Meyer lemons, traditional
Lisbon or Eureka lemons, found at supermarkets everywhere, will
work just as well.

1. In a large heavy saucepan over medium-high heat, warm 2 Tbs. of oil. Add
the shrimp and cook until they curl slightly, 2 minutes. Add ¼ cup of wine
and reduce uncovered by half, 1 to 2 minutes. Remove the mixture from the
pan and reserve.

2. Place the bottled clam juice or fish stock and 2 cups water in a large
saucepan on a back burner of the stove and maintain the heat below a
boil. Place a ladle in the pan.

3. Add the remaining 2 Tbs. oil to the saucepan you used to cook the
shrimp. Add the onions and cook over medium heat until soft, 7 minutes.
Add the rice and stir to coat the grains with oil, 3 minutes. Add the
remaining ¾ cup wine and cook, stirring, until the liquid evaporates,
1 minute. Reduce the heat to medium low and ladle in all of the hot
stock and stir well. Cover and simmer on low heat, stirring occasionally,
to prevent the risotto from sticking to the bottom of the pan. After
20 minutes, check the consistency. If it's chalky, cover and continue to
cook until the risotto is creamy, another 5 to 10 minutes. If it gets too
thick, add additional hot water, half a ladleful at a time.

continued on p. 76

- Wine pairing: Un-oaked Chardonnay
- Serve a first course of roasted red and yellow peppers and basil with a balsamic vinaigrette.
- For dessert, bake nectarines and drizzle with crème fraîche and honey.

4. While the risotto is cooking, grate 2 tsp. of zest from the lemon and squeeze out 1 Tbs. juice.

5. Remove the pan from the heat, add the shrimp, another ladle of hot water, the butter, half of the Parmigiano-Reggiano, the lemon zest, and lemon juice. Season to taste with salt and pepper. Cover and let stand for 5 minutes.

6. Remove the cover and stir. Place in serving bowls, sprinkle with the remaining Parmigiano-Reggiano, garnish with parsley, and serve immediately.

IN THE KITCHEN cooking risotto

Here's a quick and foolproof way to cook risotto. Instead of adding the stock incrementally and stirring constantly, add the stock all at once, place the cover on top of the pot, and simmer on low. Give the risotto a few stirs to prevent it from sticking to the pan. After 20 minutes, remove the risotto from the heat and add the flavorings (in this recipe, the shrimp, butter, cheese, lemon zest, and lemon juice). Let the risotto with flavorings sit, covered, for 5 minutes, then remove the cover and stir.

saffron gnocchi with pork ragu

4 cups milk

1 cup semolina

1½ tsp. saffron threads

3 Tbs. unsalted butter; more for the pan

1 cup finely grated pecorino (about 4 ounces)

1 egg, whisked

Kosher salt and freshly ground black pepper

2 Tbs. olive oil

3 ounces pancetta, chopped

1 small yellow onion, minced

¼ cup chopped fresh flat-leaf parsley

1 pound ground pork

1¼ pounds tomatoes (about 2 cups), peeled, seeded, and puréed in a blender (fresh or canned)

2 bay leaves

2 tsp. chopped fresh sage

serves 6

SERVING SUGGESTIONS

- Wine pairing: Nero d'Avola or Falanghina
- To start, serve a crispy bread topped with oven-dried tomato tapenade.
- For dessert, serve skewers of grilled pineapple dusted with cinnamon and brown sugar.

THIS RECIPE WAS INSPIRED BY MY TRAVELS AND TEACHING IN Sardinia, the awe-inspiring Mediterranean island off the western coast of Italy. The addition of saffron threads to the gnocchi dough produces the most stunning color. The salmon-hued dumplings recall the sun setting off the Sardinian coast. If I close my eyes and take a bite of these semolina gnocchi, slathered in rich pork and tomato ragu, I'm transported back to the island. A little slice of heaven.

1. Place the milk in a heavy-bottom saucepan and scald. Add the semolina and saffron and stir with a wooden spoon until stiff and thick, 20 minutes. Add the butter, ½ cup of pecorino, the egg, and salt to taste. Stir well until the butter is melted.

2. Spread the semolina mixture on your work surface to approximately ¾ inch thick. Cool for 30 minutes.

3. In the meantime, warm the oil in a large frying pan over medium heat. Add the pancetta, onions, and parsley and cook, stirring occasionally until the onions are soft, 10 minutes. Add the pork and cook, stirring occasionally, until browned, 10 minutes. Add the tomatoes, bay leaves, and sage and season with salt and pepper. Reduce the heat to low and simmer, uncovered, until the sauce thickens, 20 to 30 minutes. Remove the bay leaves and discard.

4. Heat the oven to 425°F and butter a 9 x 13-inch pan. Using a 2-inch-diameter circle cutter, cut as many circles as possible from the cooled semolina (it hardens a bit as it cools). Overlap the circles in rows in the pan until all of the semolina circles are used. Bake the gnocchi until light golden, 30 minutes.

5. To serve, pour the hot sauce over the gnocchi, garnish with the remaining ½ cup pecorino, and serve from the pan at the table.

semolina gnocchi with brown butter & fried sage

4 cups milk

1 cup semolina

9 Tbs. unsalted butter, plus more for the pan

1 cup grated Parmigiano-Reggiano

Freshly grated nutmeg

1 egg, whisked

Kosher salt

Olive oil, for frying the sage

50 sage leaves

serves 8

THESE BEAUTIFUL SEMOLINA DUMPLINGS THAT I FIRST TASTED IN Rome may be quite different from the gnocchi many are used to seeing. Rather than rolling and forming the dough, cooked semolina is spread thin on a work surface, then cut into small discs and layered in a baking dish, where they are drizzled with nutty brown butter, sprinkled with Parmigiano, and baked until golden brown. Crispy fried sage leaves then garnish the delicate gnocchi, providing the perfect woodsy crunch. Once you have made these, you, too, will be addicted!

1. Place the milk in a heavy-bottom saucepan over medium heat and scald (see p. 71). Add the semolina and stir with a wooden spoon until stiff and thick, 20 minutes. Add 3 Tbs. butter, ½ cup Parmigiano, nutmeg to taste, the egg, and salt to taste. Stir well until the butter is melted.

2. Spread the semolina mixture on your work surface to approximately ¾ inch thick. Cool for 30 minutes.

3. Heat the oven to 425°F. Using a 2-inch-diameter circle cutter, cut as many circles as possible from the cooled semolina (it hardens a bit as it cools). Butter a 9 x 11-inch pan. Overlap the circles in rows in the pan until all of the semolina circles are used.

4. Place the remaining 6 Tbs. butter in a saucepan over medium heat and cook until the foam subsides, it smells nutty, and there are golden brown bits on the bottom of the pan. Drizzle evenly over the top of the gnocchi. Sprinkle the remaining ½ cup Parmigiano-Reggiano over the top. Bake the gnocchi until light golden, 25 minutes.

continued on p. 80

- Wine pairing: Gewürztraminer or Riesling

- Start your dinner with a radicchio, Gorgonzola, and toasted hazel-nut salad.

- For dessert, serve fresh ripe melon.

5. In the meantime, heat about ½ inch olive oil in a small frying pan until it begins to ripple. Add the sage in batches and cook until deep green and crisp, 30 seconds. Remove from the pan with a slotted spoon or tongs and drain on paper towels.

6. To serve, place the gnocchi on individual serving plates, and garnish with a few fried sage leaves.

thai rice bowl with calamari salad

Kosher salt

1½ cups jasmine rice

½ pound fresh, cleaned calamari

2 shallots, thinly sliced

½ English cucumber, unpeeled, halved, seeded, and thinly sliced

1 stalk lemongrass, outer leaves removed, minced

⅓ cup coarsely chopped fresh mint

⅓ cup coarsely chopped fresh cilantro leaves and stems, plus sprigs for garnish

3 Tbs. freshly squeezed lime juice

1 Tbs. grated fresh ginger

2 Tbs. fish sauce or nam pla

1 serrano chile, seeded and minced

½ tsp. sugar

Mint sprigs, for garnish

serves 6

CALAMARI IS ONE OF THE EASIEST THINGS TO COOK. ALL IT TAKES is 30 seconds in boiling water and voilà! As long as you buy the calamari already cleaned, there is nothing to it. Tossed with myriad Thai ingredients, including lemongrass, ginger, fish sauce, and mint, and served on a bed of fragrant jasmine rice, this calamari salad is jam-packed with fresh, vibrant flavor. Toss it as you eat—you'll love it!

1. Bring 3 cups of water to a boil and add 1 tsp. salt. Add the rice, reduce the heat to low, and simmer, tightly covered, until all of the water is absorbed, 20 to 25 minutes.

2. Cut the calamari in half from top to bottom. Lay the pieces flat and score the calamari bodies by making diagonal cuts in one direction and then the opposite direction, taking care not to cut all the way through the calamari. Cut the bodies into 1-inch strips.

3. Bring a pot of salted water to a boil and add the calamari. Cook just until opaque, 30 seconds. Remove immediately with a slotted spoon. Place the cooked calamari in a medium bowl and add the shallots, cucumbers, lemongrass, mint, chopped cilantro, lime juice, ginger, fish sauce, chile, and sugar. Taste and season with salt or additional fish sauce if needed.

4. When the rice is done, remove the pan from the heat and let sit, covered, for 5 minutes. After 5 minutes, spoon the rice into individual serving bowls and top with the calamari salad, distributing evenly. Garnish with mint and cilantro sprigs.

SERVING SUGGESTIONS

- Drink pairing: Riesling or ice-cold beer
- Toss some cashews with five-spice powder, brown sugar, and cayenne and roast for 10 minutes in a 325°F oven. Serve as a starter.
- To finish the meal, serve fresh mango, pineapple, and papaya.

3
beans,
THE MIRACLE FRUIT

THE RECIPES

TECHNIQUES MADE SIMPLE

cassoulet with chicken sausages

1 pound dry white beans like Great Northern or flageolet

1 yellow onion, stuck with 6 whole cloves

½ pound thick-slice bacon, cut into ¼-inch dice

1 leg of lamb (about 2 pounds)

1 pork tenderloin (about 1¼ pounds)

Kosher salt and freshly ground black pepper

Vegetable oil, for the pan

1 pound mild chicken sausage in casings, pricked with the tines of a fork

8 cloves garlic, minced

2 Tbs. tomato paste

¾ tsp. allspice

1 cup dry, homemade, coarse breadcrumbs

serves 6 to 8

CASSOULET HAILS FROM THE LANGUEDOC REGION IN SOUTHERN France and has humble origins as a classic peasant dish. If you know the dish, you know it can often take days to make, but this version is a cinch. With alternating layers of creamy white beans, tender roasted leg of lamb and pork tenderloin, sautéed chicken sausage, and topped with crisp breadcrumbs, this dish is delicious and decadent. True to its roots as a communal dish, this cassoulet is ideal for a family dinner or informal entertaining.

1. Pick over the beans and discard any stones or debris. Place the beans in a large bowl, cover with cold water by 4 inches, and soak for 4 hours or overnight. Drain, place in a large saucepan with the onion, and cover with 2 inches of water. Simmer, uncovered, over low heat until tender, 50 to 60 minutes. Reserve the cooking liquid.

2. Heat the oven to 350°F.

3. While the beans are cooking, cook the bacon slowly in a large, ovenproof, heavy-bottom casserole dish over medium heat until the fat renders, 5 minutes. Remove with a slotted spoon and drain on paper towels; reserve the fat in pan.

4. Season the lamb and pork with salt and pepper. Place in an oiled baking pan and roast in the oven for 1¼ hours, basting with the reserved bacon fat. Remove, cool, and cut into 1-inch cubes.

5. Bring 1 inch of water to a boil in a large frying pan. Add the sausages and simmer until almost firm to the touch, 10 to 15 minutes. Cool and slice into 1-inch pieces.

- Wine pairing: Malbec
- As a simple starter, serve crostini topped with goat cheese and herbs.
- For dessert, serve red-wine poached pears with a dollop of whipped cream flavored with cardamom.

6. Place one-third of beans on the bottom of the casserole. Sprinkle with half the bacon, garlic, pork, lamb, and sausage; season with salt and pepper. Repeat with another layer, adding the last third of beans on top.

7. Combine the tomato paste, allspice, 1 tsp. salt, and the bean liquid, then pour over the casserole dish until the liquid is just below the level of the beans. Bake, uncovered, for 1½ hours. Top with breadcrumbs and continue to bake until the crumbs are golden and the cassoulet is bubbling around the edges, 30 minutes.

AT THE MARKET sausage for cassoulet

Typically cassoulet is made with pork sausages, but here I've used chicken sausages, which contain less fat and have just as much flavor. Whether you are using pork or chicken, make sure you buy a fairly mild sausage without many spices.

tuscan sausage stew with tomatoes & cannellini beans

2 cups dry cannellini beans (about 1 pound)

1½ pounds pork sausage links with garlic

2 Tbs. extra-virgin olive oil

3 cloves garlic, minced

One 28-ounce can diced tomatoes

1 sprig fresh sage

1 cup low-sodium chicken stock

Kosher salt and freshly ground black pepper

Olive oil, for frying

18 sage leaves

Extra-virgin olive oil, for drizzling

serves 6

SERVING SUGGESTIONS

- Wine pairing: Chianti
- **Start with a butter lettuce salad dressed with red-wine vinaigrette and crumbled ricotta salata.**
- **For dessert, serve espresso and biscotti.**

THIS MEAL IS ITALIAN COMFORT FOOD AT ITS BEST. SLIGHTLY PEPPERY and woodsy sage cuts through the rich, creaminess of the stewed pork sausage and cannellini beans. The result is a wonderfully balanced, yet hearty dish. But it's the crispy, fried sage leaves that make this meal something to write home about. They add the ideal textural contrast, snapping in your mouth and seasoning every bite.

1. Pick over the beans and discard any stones or debris. Place the beans in a large bowl, cover with cold water by 4 inches, and soak for 4 hours or overnight. Drain, place in a large saucepan, and cover with water. Simmer, uncovered, over low heat until tender, 50 to 60 minutes, and drain.

2. Prick the sausages with a fork. Heat a frying pan over medium heat. Add ½ cup water and the sausages and cook, turning occasionally, until the sausages are half cooked, 5 minutes. Remove from the pan and cut each link diagonally into 2 pieces.

3. Warm the 2 Tbs. olive oil in a large, wide soup pot. Add the garlic and cook, stirring, for 30 seconds. Add the tomatoes, cooked cannellini beans, sausages, sage sprig, and chicken stock; season with salt and pepper. As soon as the stew is simmering, reduce the heat to medium low, and simmer for 30 to 40 minutes. Taste and season with salt and pepper.

4. In the meantime, heat ½ inch of olive oil in a small frying pan over medium-high heat until hot. Add the sage leaves and cook until crispy and bright green, 30 to 60 seconds. Using tongs, transfer to paper towels to drain.

5. To serve, ladle the stew into bowls. Garnish with sage leaves and a drizzle of extra-virgin olive oil.

chickpea salad with herbs & castelvetrano olives

1 cup dry chickpeas (about 6 ounces)

3 to 4 Tbs. red-wine vinegar

3 cloves garlic, minced

5 Tbs. extra-virgin olive oil

Kosher salt and freshly ground black pepper

3 Tbs. mixed chopped fresh herbs, such as mint, thyme, rosemary, tarragon, oregano, and basil

2 Tbs. chopped fresh flat-leaf parsley

⅓ cup pitted Castelvetrano olives

1 small red onion, cut into ½-inch dice

1 medium red bell pepper, cut into ½-inch dice

8 ounces imported Greek feta

serves 6

SERVING SUGGESTIONS

• Wine pairing: Rosé

• Fresh tomato soup flavored with mint is a great starter.

• For dessert, bake peaches with honey and top with vanilla frozen yogurt.

THIS IS THE IDEAL DISH TO PREPARE WHEN YOU'RE CRAVING something light yet satisfying for dinner. The nutlike flavor of fiber-packed chickpeas is highlighted with a zesty, garlic-rich, red-wine vinaigrette. A heavy dose of summer herbs (raid your garden if you grow herbs!) brightens the dish, while the intensely green Castelvetrano olives add a welcome sweetness. In a pinch, this salad could be made with canned chickpeas, but the dried variety has a much better texture since they don't get mushy when cooked.

This salad can be prepared 1 day in advance and stored in the refrigerator. Bring to room temperature before serving.

1. Pick over the chickpeas and discard any stones or debris. Place the chickpeas in a bowl, cover with water by 4 inches, and soak for 4 hours or overnight. Drain, place in a large saucepan, and cover with water. Simmer, uncovered, until the skins begin to crack and the beans are tender, 45 to 60 minutes. Drain and cool.

2. In a large bowl, whisk together 3 Tbs. vinegar, the garlic, and the oil. Season with salt and pepper. Add the herbs, chickpeas, olives, onion, and red pepper and toss well. Season with salt, pepper, and additional vinegar, if needed.

3. Place on a platter, coarsely crumble the feta onto the top, and serve at room temperature.

IN THE PANTRY olives

You'll find a wide variety of olives on olive bars in most markets. I like to keep many different kinds on hand, especially Castelvetrano. You can't miss them—they're bright green and have a buttery flavor and crunchy texture. They are fantastic in this salad but equally delicious on their own.

spicy fried chickpeas
& herb salad with tzatziki

2 tsp. smoked paprika

2 tsp. ground cumin

2 tsp. ground coriander

¼ tsp. cayenne pepper

Kosher salt

6 Tbs. olive oil

Two 15-ounce cans chickpeas, rinsed, drained, and patted very dry

6 medium pita breads, 6 inches in diameter

2 Tbs. extra-virgin olive oil

1 Tbs. freshly squeezed lemon juice

½ tsp. lemon zest

25 fresh mint leaves, very coarsely chopped

1 cup fresh cilantro leaves and stems, very coarsely chopped

6 cups mixed salad greens

1 recipe Tzatziki (recipe on p. 90)

serves 6

SERVING SUGGESTIONS

- Wine pairing: Riesling or Pinot Grigio

- For a starter, I love to serve baba ghanouj with cucumber slices.

- One of my favorite simple desserts is Greek yogurt drizzled with honey and sprinkled with toasted pine nuts.

THINK OF THIS DINNER AS DECONSTRUCTED FALAFEL THAT REQUIRES just a fraction of the effort. First, chickpeas are fried in olive oil and tossed in a mixture of smoked paprika, cumin, coriander, and cayenne, creating a slightly crunchy exterior that hides a smooth, creamy interior. These spicy-hot chickpeas are then tossed with a vibrant salad of mixed greens, mint, and cilantro, stuffed inside a warm pita and drizzled with homemade tzatziki.

Save yourself a lot of time by using canned chickpeas. Just make sure they're bone-dry when you drop them into the olive oil to avoid oil spatters.

1. Heat the oven to 350°F. Combine the paprika, cumin, coriander, and cayenne in a medium-size bowl and set aside. Season with salt.

2. Heat the olive oil in a medium frying pan over medium-high heat until it begins to ripple. Working in 2 batches, add the chickpeas to the frying pan and cook, stirring frequently, until golden and crispy, 10 minutes. Using a slotted spoon, transfer the chickpeas to paper towels to drain briefly. Place in the bowl with the spices and toss to coat.

3. Wrap the pita in foil and place in the oven until warm, 10 minutes.

4. Make the dressing by whisking together the extra-virgin olive oil, lemon juice, and lemon zest in a small bowl. Season with salt. Toss the mint, cilantro, and salad greens together in a bowl with the dressing. Add the chickpeas.

5. Cut the pitas in half and open each pocket. Divide the salad between the pita pockets. Drizzle with the Tzatziki and serve immediately.

continued on p. 90

tzatziki

1 English cucumber, peeled, seeded, and finely diced

Kosher salt

2 cups whole milk Greek yogurt

3 to 4 cloves garlic, minced

3 Tbs. chopped fresh mint

3 Tbs. chopped fresh dill

1 Tbs. extra-virgin olive oil

1 to 3 tsp. freshly squeezed lemon juice

1. Place the cucumbers on paper towels and sprinkle lightly with salt. Let drain for 10 minutes. Using paper towels, squeeze out the excess moisture (don't worry about squishing the cucumber pieces).

2. In a medium bowl, combine the yogurt, cucumbers, garlic, mint, dill, and oil. Mix well. Add lemon juice to taste and season with salt.

AT THE MARKET cucumbers

You'll see two or three kinds of cucumbers at the market: those that are waxed and the long skinny English cucumbers that are wrapped in plastic wrap. I prefer the English variety because they have fewer seeds, better flavor, and less water. The English variety costs more, but what you gain for the price is quality. Also, Persian cucumbers, a smaller variety, are excellent quality.

lentil, bacon & potato salad with mustard dressing

1½ cups French lentils

½ pound fingerling or small Yukon Gold potatoes

6 large eggs

4 strips thick-slice apple-smoked bacon (about 4 ounces), cut into ½-inch pieces

1 clove garlic, minced

5 Tbs. extra-virgin olive oil

3 Tbs. red-wine vinegar

1 Tbs. Dijon mustard

Kosher salt and freshly ground black pepper

4 green onions, white and green parts, thinly sliced

1 stalk celery, cut into ¼-inch dice

Fresh flat-leaf parsley, for garnish

serves 6

THE HEAVENLY DIJON VINAIGRETTE IN THIS SALAD IS ONE YOU'LL make time and again. The base has a touch of bacon fat, adding a distinctly smoky bacon flavor to the salad that pairs well with hearty lentils. And I love this dressing so much that when I make it, sometimes I double the recipe and save it in the refrigerator for another salad. Or if you have bacon left over from breakfast, crumble it and use a little of the bacon fat to make this salad. Little tricks like this make cooking so much easier and give you confidence in the kitchen.

1. Pick over the lentils and discard any stones. Place the lentils in a large saucepan and cover with water by 2 inches. Bring to a boil, reduce the heat to low, and simmer until the lentils are tender, 25 to 35 minutes.

2. In the meantime, bring a medium-size saucepan of water to a boil. Add the potatoes and cook until they're tender and can be easily pierced with a fork, 15 to 20 minutes. Drain and cool. Cut the potatoes in half.

3. While the potatoes are cooking, hard-boil the eggs (see the sidebar on p. 92). Peel the eggs and cut in half.

4. Place the bacon in a large frying pan over medium heat. Cook, turning occasionally, until the bacon is golden and crisp, 5 to 6 minutes. With a slotted spoon, remove the bacon and drain on paper towels.

5. Remove the pan from the heat and let it cool for 5 minutes. Drain all but 1 Tbs. of the bacon fat from the pan. Add the garlic, oil, vinegar, and mustard to the pan and whisk together. Season with salt and pepper.

continued on p. 92

- Wine pairing: Cava or Prosecco
- To start, make a creamy roasted cauliflower soup flavored with ground coriander.
- For dessert, sauté some apples with brown sugar and top them with crushed ginger cookie crumbs.

6. Drain the lentils and discard the water. Add the vinaigrette, bacon, potatoes, green onions, and celery to the warm lentils and toss together.

7. Place in a large serving bowl and tuck the eggs around the edges. Sprinkle pepper on the eggs and garnish with parsley.

IN THE KITCHEN cooking hard-boiled eggs

In salads, I like my hard-boiled eggs to have a slightly soft, bright yellow, creamy yolk. Here is the best way to do this: Bring a saucepan of water to a boil. Fill a large bowl with ice cubes and water (making an ice bath) and set next to the stove. With a slotted spoon, lower the eggs, one at a time, into the boiling water. Reduce the heat to medium and cook the eggs for 8 minutes exactly. Remove the eggs and add to the ice bath, submersing them. After 1 minute, the eggs will be cool enough to handle.

Remove from the ice bath and crack all over. Return them to the ice bath for 5 minutes. By cracking the shells of the cooked eggs and returning them to the ice bath, you allow water to seep under the skin, loosening the shells so that they're a cinch to peel. By using this method, you will have perfectly cooked eggs.

summer bean salad with shrimp, mint & chive oil

¾ cup fresh shelling beans

Kosher salt and freshly ground black pepper

½ cup plus ½ tsp. extra-virgin olive oil

1½ pounds extra large shrimp (26 to 30 count), peeled, deveined, and tails left on

¾ pound green beans, cut into 1½-inch pieces

25 fresh mint leaves, plus mint sprigs (for garnish)

¼ cup coarsely chopped fresh chives

1 tsp. freshly squeezed lemon juice

1 small head frisée or 3 cups mixed salad greens

Lemon wedges, for garnish

serves 6

WHEN I THINK ABOUT COMPOSING A RECIPE, I THINK ABOUT SURPRISING your palate and taste buds with contrasting flavors, texture, and even colors. That's what makes simple cooking interesting. This salad combines the creamy texture and subtle earthiness of fresh shell beans with tender green beans and broiled prawns. Add a silky smooth herb oil, made with fresh, crisp mint and snappy chives, and top it with a salad of bitter, wiry frisée, and your palate is in for a treat. What you will love is the impressive array of flavors and textures that announce summertime.

1. Place the shelling beans in a large saucepan and cover with water by 2 inches. Simmer over low heat until they crack just slightly when you blow on them, 30 to 40 minutes. Drain, place in a large bowl, toss with salt, pepper, and 1 Tbs. of the oil, and cool.

2. Heat the broiler and position the oven rack 5 inches from the heat source.

3. Place the shrimp on a baking sheet. Toss with 2 Tbs. of the oil and spread them out into a single layer. Season with salt and pepper. Broil the shrimp for 1 to 1½ minutes, depending on their size, then turn and broil for another 1 to 1½ minutes until they are pink and slightly firm to the touch. Add to the bowl of shelling beans.

4. Bring a saucepan of salted water to a boil over high heat. Add the green beans and simmer until tender, 4 to 6 minutes. Drain. Add to the shelling beans and shrimp.

continued on p. 94

- Wine pairing: Un-oaked Chardonnay or Sauvignon Blanc

- For a first course, serve a simple pasta al brodo, which is nothing more than a handful of tiny pasta cooked in a flavorful chicken broth, sprinkled with Parmigiano-Reggiano, and drizzled with extra-virgin olive oil.

- Finish the meal by serving pitted and halved cherries, topped with a dollop of sweetened sour cream and toasted pecan pieces.

5. In the meantime, bring a small pot of water to a boil. Add the mint leaves and blanch for 20 seconds. Drain. Place the mint leaves and chives in a blender or food processor and purée. With the motor running, slowly add 5 Tbs. of oil and process for 30 seconds. Scrape down the sides and continue to purée until the mixture is smooth, 30 to 60 seconds. Add the purée to the shrimp and beans and toss together. Season with salt and pepper.

6. Whisk the remaining 1 tsp. oil and lemon juice together. Season with salt and pepper. Toss with the frisée.

7. Mound the beans and shrimp on a large platter and top with the frisée. Garnish with mint sprigs and lemon wedges, and serve immediately.

AT THE MARKET shelling beans

Toward the later part of summer, fresh shelling beans are available at most farmers' markets. They are usually sold in the pod, but I have found them shelled, which can save some time. If they are still in the pod, it's easy enough to remove the pod (and discard it). Fresh shelling beans are much easier to cook than dry beans since they only need to be simmered for about 20 to 30 minutes; dry beans need to be soaked and then simmered for double that amount of time.

ham & lentil soup
with mint & tomatoes

1 cup French green lentils (about 7 ounces)

1 Tbs. extra-virgin olive oil

1 medium yellow onion, chopped

3 cloves garlic, minced

3 fresh mint sprigs plus 5 Tbs. chopped fresh mint (for garnish)

1 large smoked ham hock, about 1 pound

1½ cups peeled, seeded, and chopped tomatoes (fresh or canned)

6 cups chicken stock

Kosher salt and freshly ground black pepper

serves 6

SERVING SUGGESTIONS

- Wine pairing: Beaujolais
- Start dinner with an endive, toasted almond, and blue cheese salad.
- For dessert, serve baked apples topped with a dollop of crème fraîche and drizzled with maple syrup.

LENTILS AND HAM ARE A CLASSIC COMBINATION, BUT THIS SOUP notches up the flavor with fresh mint. And it's good for you, too, thanks to the lentils. They are easier to work with than other dry beans because they don't have to be soaked and they cook in much less time. I prefer using the small imported French lentils that range from dark emerald green to chocolate brown as opposed to the larger American lentils that tend to fall apart when simmered.

1. Pick over the lentils and discard any stones or debris. Place the lentils in a large saucepan and cover with water. Bring to a boil, reduce the heat to low, and simmer until the lentils are tender, 30 to 35 minutes. Drain.

2. Warm the oil in a soup pot over medium heat. Add the onions and cook, stirring occasionally, until the onions are soft, 10 minutes. Add the garlic and continue to cook for 1 minute. With the back of a knife, tap the stems of the mint sprigs to release their flavor, then use kitchen string to tie them into a bundle. Add the mint to the pan along with the ham hock, tomatoes, and chicken stock. Reduce the heat to low and simmer until the meat begins to fall off the bone, 1 hour.

3. Add the lentils and continue to simmer for 30 minutes. Remove and discard the mint sprigs. Remove the ham hocks; pull any remaining ham off the bones, then discard the skin and bones. Cut the ham into bite-size pieces and add to the soup. Season to taste with salt and pepper. Ladle the soup into bowls and garnish with chopped mint.

AT THE MARKET ham hocks

Most markets carry ham hocks. Reasonably priced, one ham hock adds a distinctive smoky flavor to a finished dish. Since ham hocks usually consist of skin, tendons, and ligaments, long cooking time is required. If they aren't available, a smoked turkey leg will make a good substitute.

spanish beans
with chorizo

1 pound large navy beans

4 Tbs. olive oil

1½ pounds pork shoulder, cut into
1-inch chunks, excess fat removed

½ pound firm semidry chorizo, cut
into ¼-inch slices

1 yellow onion, finely chopped

1 green pepper, cut into ½-inch dice

4 cloves garlic, minced

1 tsp. sweet paprika

1 tsp. pimentón

1 cup peeled, seeded, and puréed
tomatoes (fresh or canned)

Kosher salt and freshly
ground pepper

Fresh flat-leaf parsley leaves,
for garnish

serves 6

SERVING SUGGESTIONS

- Wine pairing: Tempranillo
- For a simple starter, place a
  variety of olives in a pan with a few
  crumbled bay leaves, lemon zest,
  crushed red pepper flakes, and a
  sprig or two of rosemary. Drizzle
  with olive oil and heat until warm.
  Place in a serving bowl and serve
  the olives warm.
- For dessert, make a Spanish cheese
  platter of Manchego, Spanish
  sheep's milk cheese, and a wedge
  of Cabrales, a blue cheese.

THIS STEW IS FILLED WITH BOLD SPANISH FLAVORS AND IS A TRUE
fiesta on your palate. Although the cooking time for this dish is
lengthy, this is a no-fuss dinner that practically prepares itself.
Double the recipe to make a batch to freeze; it will keep for 2 months.

You'll need to plan ahead for this dish, since the beans need to
soak overnight.

1. Pick over the beans and discard any that are damaged as well as any
stones or debris. Place the beans in a large bowl, cover with cold water by
4 inches, and soak for 4 hours or overnight. Drain the beans.

2. In a large, heavy, soup pot, warm the oil over medium-high heat. Add
the pork and chorizo and cook until the meats are light golden, about
10 minutes. Reduce the heat to medium, add the onions and pepper, and
cook until the onions are soft, 8 minutes. Add the garlic, paprika, and
pimentón and continue to cook for 2 minutes.

3. Add the tomatoes, ½ tsp. salt, ¼ tsp. pepper, the beans, and 6 cups
water. Increase the heat to high and bring to a boil, then reduce the heat
to low. Simmer slowly, uncovered, until the beans are tender and the pork
cubes can be easily skewered and the meat begins to fall apart, 1½ to
2 hours. Add additional water as needed if the beans start to pop through
the top of the water and look dry. Taste and season with salt and pepper.

4. To serve, ladle the stew into bowls and garnish with parsley.

IN THE KITCHEN sorting beans

To sort beans, spread them out
on a baking sheet. Pick out and
keep those that are blemish free
and not split. Toss any that are
wrinkled or damaged.

spiced split pea & carrot soup

½ cup yellow or orange split peas, about 3 ounces

3 Tbs. olive oil

1 small yellow onion, coarsely chopped

1 tsp. ground coriander

1 tsp. ground cumin

½ tsp. ground cardamom

1 Tbs. grated fresh ginger

4 medium carrots, peeled and coarsely chopped

4 cups chicken stock

Kosher salt and freshly ground black pepper

1 Tbs. coriander seeds

⅓ cup Greek yogurt

3 Tbs. chopped fresh cilantro, plus 6 sprigs (for garnish)

serves 6

THIS SOUP IS VELVETY SMOOTH AND BEAUTIFULLY SEASONED WITH fresh ginger and lots of aromatic dried spices like coriander, cumin, and cardamom. Spices add so much depth to a dish. Just imagine how lovely your kitchen will smell with those aromatics bubbling away on your stovetop. On its own, the soup is delicious, but finished with a simple drizzle of exotic coriander oil and a dollop of cilantro yogurt, it's over the top.

1. Pick over the split peas and discard any damaged peas, stones, or debris. Rinse the peas and drain.

2. In a soup pot over medium heat, warm 1 Tbs. of oil. Add the onions, coriander, cumin, cardamom, and ginger and cook, stirring occasionally, until the onions are soft, 8 to 10 minutes. Add the carrots, stock, 4 cups water, and split peas; bring to a boil, reduce the heat to low, and simmer gently until the split peas are completely soft, 30 to 40 minutes.

3. Remove the soup from the heat and let cool for 30 minutes. Working in small batches, purée the soup in a blender on high speed until smooth, about 2 minutes per batch. Thin with water or stock if the soup is too thick. Return the soup to a clean pan. Season with salt and pepper.

IN THE KITCHEN toasting spices

The best way to bring out the flavor of spices is to "toast" them. To do this, set a dry frying pan on medium-high heat and warm it for about 15 seconds. Add the spices and shake the pan until the spices are aromatic. Don't let them take on any color. Grind the spices in an electric spice or coffee grinder or in a mortar and pestle.

- Wine pairing: Riesling
- A warm goat cheese salad is a perfect starter.
- To finish the meal, make a puff pastry tart with pears and ginger. Buy puff pastry, roll it out, and cut it into an 11-inch circle. Crimp the edges and top it with pears, sugar, and freshly grated ginger. Serve the tart warm with softly whipped cream or store-bought vanilla ice cream.

4. Crush the coriander seeds in a mortar and pestle, coffee grinder, or spice grinder until they are coarsely ground. If using a coffee grinder or spice grinder, pulse a few times only. Place the coriander and remaining 2 Tbs. olive oil in a saucepan over medium heat. Warm for 1 minute and remove from the heat. In a small bowl, stir together the yogurt, chopped cilantro, and enough water to make a barely fluid paste. Season with salt.

5. Before serving, reheat the soup gently. Ladle the soup into bowls, drizzle with the coriander oil and yogurt, and serve immediately, garnished with 1 cilantro sprig per bowl.

IN THE KITCHEN peeling fresh ginger

Freshly grated ginger adds a delicious punch to a dish. I always have a piece of fresh ginger on hand to use in a variety of dishes. To peel it, hold the ginger in one hand and a spoon in the other. With the front side of the tip of the spoon resting against the ginger, scrape the tip of the spoon along the ginger, removing the skin. You can also use a knife to peel the skin, but you lose a lot of the ginger. Once the ginger is peeled, either use a Microplane® to finely grate the ginger or finely dice it for use.

succotash salad

3 ears fresh sweet corn on the cob, husked and halved

1 cup fresh shelling beans or ¾ pound frozen baby lima beans

Kosher salt and freshly ground black pepper

1 pound green beans and/or yellow wax beans, cut into 1-inch lengths

1 medium zucchini, cut into ½-inch dice

1 medium red bell pepper, cut into ½-inch dice

½ red onion, cut into ½-inch dice

2½ Tbs. freshly squeezed lemon juice

2 Tbs. extra-virgin olive oil

2 Tbs. canola oil

3 Tbs. torn fresh basil leaves

serves 6

SERVING SUGGESTIONS

- Wine pairing: Sauvignon Blanc or Albarino

- Serve with cornbread and a bowl of chilled gazpacho for a perfect summertime meal.

THE TWO ESSENTIAL SUCCOTASH ELEMENTS, SWEET CORN AND shelling beans, are joined by green beans, red bell pepper, and zucchini. This light main dish salad is as simple as cooking the vegetables in boiling water until just tender and tossing them in a tart lemon dressing. Red onions add a nice crisp bite, while torn fresh basil leaves lend a beautiful freshness to the dish.

1. Bring a large saucepan of water to a boil. Add the corn and simmer, uncovered, until the kernels turn slightly darker yellow, 5 to 6 minutes. With tongs, remove the corn from the water and let cool. Cut the kernels off the cobs (see sidebar on p. 41); discard the cobs and reserve the kernels.

2. Bring the saucepan of water to a boil again. Add the fresh shelling beans and simmer until tender, 25 to 30 minutes. If you are using frozen lima beans, simmer for 5 minutes. Remove with a slotted spoon and cool.

3. Bring the same saucepan of water to a boil. Add 1 tsp. salt and the string or wax beans and simmer until almost tender but still very crisp, about 4 minutes. Add the zucchini and simmer for an additional 2 minutes. Drain and cool.

4. Place the butter or lima beans, string or wax beans, corn, zucchini, peppers, and onions in a large bowl.

5. In a small bowl, whisk together the lemon juice, olive oil, and canola oil. Season with salt and pepper. Add the dressing and basil to the bean and corn mixture and stir together. Place the salad in a large serving bowl and serve.

summer vegetable stew with basil & mint pesto

½ cup dry cannellini beans

6 Tbs. extra-virgin olive oil

1 small yellow onion, chopped

2 small carrots, peeled and cut into ½-inch dice

2 small stalks celery, cut into ½-inch dice

2 cups tomatoes, peeled, seeded, and chopped (fresh or canned)

4 cups chicken stock

1 cup packed fresh basil leaves, washed and dried

¼ cup fresh mint leaves, washed and dried

1 Tbs. toasted pine nuts

1 clove garlic, minced

1 cup grated Parmigiano-Reggiano

Kosher salt and freshly ground black pepper

½ pound green beans, ends trimmed and cut into 1-inch lengths diagonally

¼ pound fusilli

3 cups lightly packed Swiss chard leaves (about 1 small bunch), cut into 1-inch pieces

serves 8

THERE ARE SO MANY THINGS TO LOVE ABOUT THIS SOUP. FIRST, IT'S chock full of fresh vegetables and so vitamin-rich, I'm convinced my skin glows and hair shines just from breathing in the steam as it simmers. And the pesto with its crisp, fresh flavor of mint and basil practically dances on your tongue. But the best part is this: It's enormously versatile, so you can use your favorite combination of seasonal vegetables.

With all of the chopping involved, this soup provides ample opportunity to hone your knife skills—the single most important thing you can do to gain confidence in the kitchen. For more on this, see the sidebar on p. 105.

1. Pick over the beans and discard any stones, debris, or damaged beans. Place the beans in a large bowl, cover with cold water by 4 inches, and soak for 4 hours or overnight. Drain, place in a large saucepan, and cover with water. Simmer, uncovered, over low heat until the beans are tender and the skins just begin to crack, 45 to 60 minutes. Drain the beans.

2. Heat 2 Tbs. oil in a large soup pot over medium-low heat. Add the onions, carrots, and celery and cook, stirring occasionally, until the vegetables are tender, 20 minutes. Add the tomatoes, stock, and 3 cups of water and simmer for 45 minutes.

3. In the meantime, place the basil, mint, pine nuts, garlic, the remaining 4 Tbs. oil, and ½ cup Parmigiano-Reggiano in a blender or food processor. Blend at high speed until well mixed, 1 minute. Stop and scrape down the sides periodically and continue to blend until smooth, 1 minute. Season with salt and pepper.

continued on p. 104

- Wine pairing: Sauvignon Blanc or Pinot Gris

- To begin the meal, serve a tomato and basil salad drizzled with balsamic vinegar and extra-virgin olive oil and topped with whole basil leaves.

- For dessert, soften your favorite flavor of ice cream. Using your favorite cookie, place a layer of softened ice cream in the center and sandwich the cookies together. Wrap carefully in plastic wrap and place in the freezer for an hour. Serve the ice cream sandwiches straight from the freezer.

4. About 15 minutes before serving, add the cooked cannellini beans, green beans, and pasta to the soup pot with the vegetables and simmer, covered, until the pasta is completely cooked, 8 to 10 minutes. Add the Swiss chard and simmer until it wilts, 5 minutes. Season with salt and pepper.

5. Ladle the soup into bowls and top with a large spoonful of the pesto. Sprinkle with the remaining ½ cup Parmigiano and serve immediately.

IN THE PANTRY Parmigiano-Reggiano and Grana Padano

Domestically produced hard grating cheeses do not taste like Parmigiano-Reggiano or Grana Padano because they are produced with different raw materials using different production and aging methods. If you want the finest quality and authentic taste of Italian grating cheese, you will be the happiest when you buy Parmigiano-Reggiano and Grana Padano.

Because they are both hard grating cheeses, Parmigiano and Grana Padano can usually be substituted for one another.

chopping onions

Chopping onions is one technique every cook should master. Once you get the hang of it, you might even find it relaxing!

Cut off the stem end of the onion, peel it, and then cut the peeled onion in half, from cut end to root end. Working with one half cut side down, slice through the onion in a sawing motion, stopping before you reach the root end. Try to keep the slices as even as possible.

Reposition the onion and cut perpendicular slices through the onion, forming dice. Be sure the slices are as even as possible to ensure similar-size dice.

Use the blade of the knife to separate the diced onions from the slices.

30-minute lamb & 3-bean chili

2 Tbs. extra-virgin olive oil

1 large onion, chopped

4 Tbs. mild chili powder

3 Tbs. ground cumin

5 large cloves garlic, minced

1½ pounds grass-fed lean
ground lamb

1 serrano or jalapeño pepper,
halved, seeded, and
membranes removed

4 cups peeled, seeded, chopped
tomatoes (fresh or canned)

1 cup full-flavored beer

One 15-ounce can black beans,
drained and rinsed

One 15-ounce can white beans,
drained and rinsed

One 15-ounce can pinto beans,
drained and rinsed

Kosher salt and freshly
ground pepper

1 to 1½ cups grated sharp Cheddar,
for garnish

Diced red onions, for garnish

Lime wedges, for garnish

Tortilla chips, for garnish

serves 6

THERE'S NOTHING BETTER THAN A WARM BOWL OF CHILI ON A COLD winter night (or summer, if you live in San Francisco). This chili comes together quickly, yet it tastes as if it simmered all day. My secret? Canned beans, a fresh serrano pepper that provides the right amount of heat, and beer, which adds depth of flavor. My meat of choice in this dish is grass-fed ground lamb, but beef or turkey would work, too. If you don't see any ground lamb in the butcher case, ask your butcher to grind some for you from the leg and/or shoulder.

1. Heat the oil in a large, heavy, soup pot over medium-high heat. Add the onions, chili powder, and cumin and cook, stirring occasionally until the onions are soft, 8 to 10 minutes. Add the garlic and cook for 1 minute. Add the lamb and cook until it changes from red to brown. Add the serrano or jalapeño pepper, the tomatoes, beer, and beans.

2. Simmer slowly, uncovered, until the flavors meld and the lamb is cooked, 20 minutes. Season with salt and pepper.

3. Ladle the chili into bowls and serve garnished with Cheddar, red onions, lime wedges, and tortilla chips (or pass the garnishes at the table).

SERVING SUGGESTIONS

- Drink pairing: Ice cold beer or Mexican cola

- Start your meal with mango salsa with tortilla chips.

- For dessert, caramelize bananas in a frying pan with butter and brown sugar. To serve, place them on a plate and drizzle with warm chocolate sauce scented with cinnamon.

IN THE PANTRY dried beans

Black, black-eyed, garbanzo, Great Northern, kidney, lentils, lima, navy, pinto, and split peas can be stored in plastic or glass containers for several years. If beans are stored for long periods of time, they dry out, so I use them within a year. If beans do dry out, it will take longer to reconstitute them. You may have to soak them longer or cook them longer as well.

tuna & white bean salad with basil & tomatoes

5 Tbs. red-wine vinegar

5 Tbs. extra-virgin olive oil

Kosher salt and freshly ground black pepper

Three 6-ounce cans white albacore tuna, packed in olive oil, drained

Two 15-ounce cans cannellini beans

1 small red onion, finely diced

1½ cups mix of red and yellow cherry tomatoes, halved

¼ cup fresh basil leaves, cut into chiffonade

serves 6

SERVING SUGGESTIONS

- Wine pairing: Sauvignon Blanc
- As an option, serve the tuna-bean salad open-faced on a toasted piece of artisanal bread or nestled in a bed of mixed greens.
- For dessert, serve grilled figs with mascarpone.

THIS TUNA SALAD IS A REFRESHING DEPARTURE FROM THE TRADITIONAL mayonnaise-based variety. A simple red-wine vinaigrette brings a crisp acidity to the salad, highlighting the tuna's flavor. The sharp red onions, juicy cherry tomatoes, and aromatic basil add just a hint of Mediterranean flare.

1. In a bowl, whisk together the vinegar and oil. Season with salt and pepper.

2. With a fork, flake the tuna and add to the dressing along with the beans, red onions, cherry tomatoes, and basil. Taste and season with additional salt and pepper if needed.

IN THE KITCHEN grilling tuna

In place of canned tuna, you can also use grilled fresh tuna. To grill tuna, brush both sides with olive oil and grill the tuna 4 inches from the heat source set on high. Grill until the tuna has grill marks but the inside is still pink, 2 to 3 minutes per side. Season with salt and pepper. Remove from the grill and let cool. Tear the tuna into rough 1-inch pieces.

pinto bean, roasted corn & avocado tostada with tomatillo salsa

1 cup dry pinto beans

2 ears fresh corn on the cob

2 cups drained, canned tomatillos (about 24 ounces), diced

6 Tbs. chopped fresh cilantro, plus sprigs (for garnish)

¼ cup minced red onions

2 Tbs. freshly squeezed lime juice

½ to 1 whole fresh jalapeño or serrano chile, seeded and minced

Kosher salt and freshly ground black pepper

2 ripe avocados

¾ cup sour cream

1½ tsp. minced chipotle in adobo

1 cup corn oil

6 corn tortillas (6 inches in diameter)

3 cups romaine, washed and thinly sliced

serves 6

THIS TOSTADA IS A LIGHT AND FRESH WAY TO ENJOY DELICIOUS Mexican flavors. The grilled corn adds a wonderful smoky flavor to the creamy pinto beans, which are piled high on a crispy fried corn tortilla. Topped with romaine lettuce, avocado, homemade tomatillo salsa, and a dollop of sour cream, this dish is the perfect mixture of healthy and indulgent, as each bite satisfies with a touch of crunchy fried goodness from the tostada.

1. Pick over and discard any damaged beans, stones, or debris. Place the beans in a large bowl, cover with cold water by 4 inches, and let soak for about 3 hours. Drain, place in a large saucepan, and cover with water. Bring to a boil, reduce the heat to low, and simmer, uncovered, until tender, 35 to 45 minutes. Drain and set aside in a bowl.

2. In the meantime, heat an outdoor grill. Remove half of the husks from the corn so that half of the kernels are revealed. Grill the corn 4 inches from the coals or heating element, turning the cobs occasionally, until the corn husks and corn kernels are golden brown, 8 to 10 minutes. Remove the husks and silk and discard. Cut the kernels from the cob and set aside.

3. In a bowl, mix together the tomatillos, chopped cilantro, red onions, lime juice, and chiles. Add the corn and beans and toss together. Season with salt and pepper.

4. Working with one avocado at a time, cut the avocado from top to bottom, going right around the pit. Twist the two pieces to separate the halves. Tap the blade of your knife into the pit to lodge the blade in the pit. Twist the blade and remove the pit from the avocado, then remove the pit from the knife (be careful of the knife—the pit can be slippery). With a large spoon, scoop the pulp away from the skin. Discard the pit and skin. Cut the avocado into ½-inch chunks.

continued on p. 110

- Drink pairing: Margaritas or ice-cold beer

- As a starter, serve cucumber and jicama sticks drizzled with freshly squeezed lime juice, salt, and a good pinch of crushed red pepper flakes or ground adobo.

- For dessert, serve fruit salad with honey, lime juice, and toasted pumpkin seeds.

5. In a bowl, combine the sour cream and chipotle. Season with salt.

6. Just before serving, heat the oil in a frying pan over medium-high heat until almost rippling. Add the tortillas one at a time and cook until light golden and almost crisp on both sides, 1 to 2 minutes. Drain on paper towels.

7. To serve, place one crispy tortilla on each plate. Top with the bean and corn mixture, distributing it evenly. Top with romaine, avocado chunks, a dollop of chipotle sour cream, and cilantro sprigs, distributing the ingredients evenly among the tostadas.

IN THE KITCHEN know your knives

My students are always asking me what kinds of knives they need to buy. I recommend 4 basic knives: a 9-inch chef's knife, a serrated knife, a 6-inch chef's knife, and a 4-inch paring knife. You can do almost everything with these.

A dull knife is more dangerous than a sharp knife, so to keep your knives in tip-top shape, buy a diamond steel. To hone your knives, hold the blade at a 20-degree angle and sharpen both sides of the knife blade from top to bottom. Once a year, it's best to have your knives sharpened professionally.

farro, white bean & kale stew

1½ cups dry cannellini beans (about 10 ounces)

2 Tbs. extra-virgin olive oil, plus more for drizzling

¼ pound pancetta in 1 piece, cut into ¼-inch dice

1 medium yellow onion, diced

1 large carrot, peeled and cut into ¼-inch dice

1 stalk celery, cut into ¼-inch dice

1 sprig fresh rosemary

2 cloves garlic, minced

1 cup farro (about 6 ounces)

1 bunch kale, leaves and ribs, cut into 1-inch pieces

4 cups chicken stock

Kosher salt and freshly ground black pepper

serves 8

SERVING SUGGESTIONS

- Wine pairing: Beaujolais Villages or Pinot Grigio

- To accompany the stew, toast some bread, rub with a whole clove of garlic, brush with extra-virgin olive oil, and drape a slice of prosciutto on top.

- For dessert, serve a big bowl of fresh fruit and your favorite cookie.

THIS IS MY GO-TO DISH WHENEVER I FEEL LIKE I'VE OVERINDULGED during the holidays. Not only is this stew packed with nutritious ingredients, but it's downright delicious. The pancetta and rosemary add a wonderful depth of flavor, while puréeing a portion of the beans gives the stew the most beautiful velvety texture.

1. Pick over the beans and discard any stones or debris. Place the beans in a large bowl, cover with cold water by 4 inches, and soak for 4 hours or overnight. Drain the beans, place in a large saucepan, and cover with water. Simmer, uncovered, over low heat until tender, 45 to 60 minutes. Drain the beans, reserving the cooking liquid. Purée about half the beans with the cooking liquid to make a smooth paste. Set aside.

2. In a large soup pot over medium heat, warm the 2 Tbs. of olive oil. Add the pancetta and cook just until it starts to turn golden, 3 to 4 minutes. Add the onions, carrots, celery, rosemary, and garlic and cook, stirring occasionally, until the vegetables are soft, 10 to 12 minutes.

3. Add the farro, the bean purée, the kale, 2 cups of water, and chicken stock. Bring to a boil, then reduce the heat to low and simmer for 15 minutes. Add the whole beans and continue to cook until the farro and kale are tender and the soup is thick, 45 to 50 minutes. Season to taste with salt and pepper.

4. Ladle into bowls, drizzle with olive oil, and serve immediately.

IN THE KITCHEN dicing bacon or pancetta

A great little trick for dicing bacon or pancetta is to freeze it for 10 minutes prior to dicing. It's much easier to cut when it's a bit firm rather than trying to dice it while it's at a slippery room temperature.

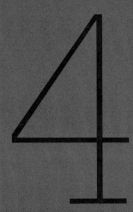

4

NOT YOUR AVERAGE

chicken

RECIPES

THE RECIPES

TECHNIQUES MADE SIMPLE

chicken breasts stuffed with goat cheese, arugula & lemon

5 ounces fresh goat cheese

2 Tbs. milk

2 cloves garlic, minced

²/₃ cup chopped fresh arugula

1 Tbs. grated lemon zest

Pinch of crushed red pepper flakes

Kosher salt and freshly ground black pepper

6 boneless, skinless chicken breast halves, about 6 ounces each

2 Tbs. extra-virgin olive oil

1 cup dry white wine, such as Sauvignon Blanc

1 cup low-sodium chicken stock

serves 6

ONE OF THE BEST WAYS TO JAZZ UP BONELESS, SKINLESS CHICKEN breasts is to stuff them. Here, that stuffing is a mixture of tangy goat cheese, peppery arugula, and fresh-tasting lemon zest. The mixture seasons the chicken from the inside out and melts beautifully as the chicken cooks, providing a touch of flavorful creaminess with every bite.

The simple pan sauce that finishes the dish is one that can be used anytime you cook meat in a pan. You'll make it by deglazing the pan with wine, a technique every cook should have in his or her back pocket.

1. In a small bowl, mash together the goat cheese and milk until smooth. Add the garlic, arugula, lemon zest, and red pepper flakes. Season to taste with salt and pepper.

2. On the thickest side of each chicken breast, cut a deep, 3-inch-long pocket. (Be sure you don't cut through the other side of the breast.) Using your fingers, stuff the goat cheese mixture into each pocket. Close by pressing the flesh together and secure with a toothpick, if necessary.

3. In a large frying pan, heat the oil over medium heat. Have ready a lid that is too small for the pan but that will cover the breasts. Cook the chicken on one side, uncovered, until golden brown, 4 to 5 minutes. Turn the breasts, season with salt and pepper, and set the small lid on top of the chicken in the pan. Continue to cook until the chicken is cooked through, 4 to 5 minutes more.

continued on p. 116

SERVING SUGGESTIONS

- Wine pairing: Sauvignon Blanc
- As a side dish with the chicken, serve steamed broccoli flavored with lemon and garlic and/or mashed potatoes with olive oil.

4. Transfer the chicken to a serving platter. Pour the wine into the pan and scrape up the flavorful brown bits stuck to the bottom of the pan. Cook over medium heat until the wine has reduced by about half, 1 to 2 minutes. Add the chicken stock, season with salt and pepper, and cook until the sauce is reduced to a glossy syrup, 2 to 3 minutes. Drizzle the reduction over the chicken and serve.

IN THE KITCHEN stuffing chicken breasts

Stuffing chicken breasts looks harder than it is. Using a knife, cut a small pocket into the side of the breast, making sure that you cut from top to bottom so that the pocket is large enough to stuff. Stuffing gives the chicken a lot of flavor and moisture, so try lots of variations. I like olive tapenade, sun-dried tomato tapenade, mashed feta with olives and oregano, and wilted chopped spinach and fontina.

stir-fried chicken & mushroom lettuce wraps

2 Tbs. peanut oil

1 pound ground chicken (thigh meat could be substituted)

6 ounces button mushrooms, sliced

2 tsp. cornstarch

5 green onions, white and green parts, minced

⅔ cup water chestnuts, chopped

1 Tbs. grated fresh ginger

3 Tbs. soy sauce

1 Tbs. oyster sauce

¼ cup toasted pine nuts

1 large head butter lettuce, leaves separated

serves 6

I FIND THAT HOME COOKS OFTEN SHY AWAY FROM COOKING ASIAN-inspired meals. While some Asian dishes require a host of exotic ingredients, stir-frying is one of the simplest and fastest cooking techniques out there. The trick is to have all of your ingredients ready before you start cooking. Once the components hit the sizzling hot wok or frying pan, dinner is just minutes away!

This dish combines healthy ground chicken with green onions, mushrooms, and water chestnuts and is seasoned with fresh ginger, soy sauce, and oyster sauce. The mouth-watering mixture is then wrapped in crisp butter lettuce leaves for a fast, fresh, weeknight meal.

1. Warm the oil in a frying pan or wok over medium-high heat. Add the chicken, mushrooms, cornstarch, and green onions and cook, stirring constantly, until the chicken is cooked and broken into pieces, 3 to 4 minutes. Add the water chestnuts, ginger, soy sauce, and oyster sauce and cook for 1 minute. Add the pine nuts and toss together. Remove from the heat.

2. To serve, place 12 large leaves of lettuce, stem side down, on a serving plate. Working with one leaf at a time, spoon a heaping tablespoon of the chicken mixture into the center. Wrap the lettuce around the filling as you would a cabbage roll, and enjoy.

SERVING SUGGESTIONS

- Wine pairing: Semi-dry Riesling
- Start with ice-cold oysters topped with green onions, ginger, and soy sauce.
- Finish the meal with Asian pear wedges dusted with five-spice powder and Sichuan pepper.

chicken tagine with apricots, almonds & honey

3 chicken breasts, 6 to 8 ounces each, skinned and boned, cut in half diagonally

6 bone-in chicken thighs (about 2 pounds), skinned

2 tsp. ground ginger

2 tsp. Ras el Hanout

Large pinch of saffron

1 tsp. turmeric

¼ tsp. ground cinnamon

Kosher salt and freshly ground black pepper

3 Tbs. extra-virgin olive oil

1 red onion, diced

24 dried apricots, pitted

½ cup whole almonds in their skins

2 Tbs. honey

Fresh flat-leaf parsley sprigs, for garnish

serves 6

WITH ITS SIGHTS, FLAVORS, AND SMELLS, MOROCCO IS A VIBRANT country. On a recent trip to Marrakech, I introduced my students to this enchanting city and its culinary traditions, including the art of cooking a tagine, a classic Moroccan stew named for the conical clay vessel in which it is cooked. The vessel's shape allows steam to condense and seep back into the stew, intensifying its flavors.

There are many variations of tagine. This version is made with Ras el Hanout, a Moroccan spice blend, which means "top of the shop" in Arabic and refers to a mixture of the very best spices a spice shop has to offer. If you don't have a tagine, you can use a heavy soup pot as an alternative.

1. Place the chicken in a tagine or heavy soup pot. Sprinkle with the ginger, Ras el Hanout, saffron, turmeric, cinnamon, 1 tsp. salt, ½ tsp. pepper, the oil, and onions. Rub the ingredients into the chicken, then add 1½ cups of water. Bring to a boil, cover, and simmer slowly for 20 minutes. Add the apricots and almonds and continue to cook until the chicken is tender and the thigh meat is falling off the bone, 10 to 15 minutes.

2. Remove the tagine from the heat, spoon the chicken stew into a serving bowl and drizzle with the honey. Garnish with the parsley sprigs and serve immediately.

SERVING SUGGESTIONS

- Wine pairing: Torrontés or Gewürztraminer

- For a first course, make a sliced fresh carrot salad, scented with orange flower water, confectioners' sugar, and cinnamon.

- For dessert, serve honey ice cream topped with diced dates.

IN THE KITCHEN making your own ras el hanout

Every blend of Ras el Hanout is unique. While premade versions can be purchased, it's easy and fun to make your own blend. Classic spices used in Ras el Hanout are cardamom, clove, cinnamon, ground chile pepper, coriander, cumin, nutmeg, peppercorn, and turmeric. Mix together your favorite spices from those listed above; you can also add ginger, cayenne, or paprika. Ras el Hanout is also great tossed with almonds and baked.

pan-roasted chicken thighs with indian rub

2 tsp. black or brown mustard seeds

2 tsp. coriander seeds

1 tsp. cumin seeds

¾ tsp. fenugreek seeds

1 tsp. peppercorns

2 whole cloves

1 cardamom pod

½ cinnamon stick

Kosher salt

1 Tbs. olive oil

6 boneless chicken thighs (about 2 pounds), skinned

Plum-Ginger Chutney (recipe on the facing page)

serves 6

SERVING SUGGESTIONS

• Wine pairing: Slightly chilled Beaujolias

• As a side dish, serve jasmine rice steamed with ginger and an Indian sauce called raita, which is made with yogurt, grated cucumbers, ground coriander, fennel seeds, and cumin seeds, garlic, and cayenne.

TAKE A TRIP TO INDIA WITH THESE WONDERFULLY AROMATIC, SPICE-rubbed chicken thighs. Coated in toasted and freshly ground spices, including mustard seeds, coriander, fenugreek, and cardamom, the chicken thighs are baked until golden and served with homemade plum and ginger chutney. Made with fresh plums, grated ginger, and cinnamon, you'll be tempted to eat this chutney by the spoonful. It's also the perfect touch of sweetness to serve with a platter of Italian cheeses and nuts.

1. Place the mustard seeds, coriander seeds, cumin seeds, fenugreek seeds, peppercorns, cloves, cardamom pod, and cinnamon stick in a dry frying pan over medium-high heat. Shake the pan until the seeds just become aromatic, 30 to 60 seconds. Remove from the heat and let cool. Place in a spice grinder and grind to make a coarse dust. Stir in a large pinch of salt.

2. Heat the oven to 425°F.

3. Place the spice mixture on a plate and spread it out. Rub the chicken pieces with oil then dip them in the spice mixture, coating evenly on both sides. Put on a plate and set aside uncovered in the refrigerator for 1 hour to flavor the chicken.

4. Place the chicken thighs in a single layer with space between them on a baking sheet, meat side up. Bake in the middle of the oven for 15 minutes.

5. Heat the broiler. Place the baking sheet of thighs 5 to 6 inches from the heat source until the chicken is golden on the outside and firm to the touch, 4 to 5 minutes. Turn the thighs over and broil for another 4 to 5 minutes. Watch closely during the broiling to avoid the chicken getting too dark.

6. Place the chicken thighs on a platter and serve with the chutney at the table.

plum-ginger chutney

⅓ cup pear or cider vinegar

⅓ cup brown sugar

½ small onion, minced

½ tsp. ground cinnamon

1 Tbs. grated fresh ginger

1½ pounds fresh ripe plums, pitted and coarsely chopped

makes 1¼ cups

Place all of the ingredients in a medium saucepan over medium heat. Bring to a simmer and reduce the heat to low. Simmer until the chutney is thick, 1 to 1½ hours. The chutney is best served warm or at room temperature.

oven-seared chicken breasts with artichoke-almond salsa

FOR THE ARTICHOKE-ALMOND SALSA

6 whole artichoke hearts in brine, drained and very coarsely chopped

4 grape leaves in brine, stems removed, rinsed, and very coarsely chopped

½ cup imported green olives, such as picholine or Castelvetrano, pitted and chopped

1 clove garlic, minced

1 tsp. grated lemon zest

2 Tbs. extra-virgin olive oil

2½ Tbs. freshly squeezed lemon juice

Kosher salt and freshly ground black pepper

¼ cup whole almonds

FOR THE CHICKEN

1 Tbs. extra-virgin olive oil

6 chicken breasts (about 6 to 8 ounces each), skinless and boneless

Kosher salt and freshly ground black pepper

FOR GARNISH

Lemon wedges

serves 6

THE IDEA FOR THIS MEAL CAME FROM ONE OF MY CROSTINI RECIPES. You might not know, but I'm a crostini fanatic. If I'm having people over for dinner, you can bet your bottom dollar I'll be serving crostini when they arrive. Anyway, as I was making this particular crostini topping with toasted almonds, brined artichokes, grape leaves, and olives, I found myself tasting it over and over to ensure the flavors were just right. To be honest, I just kept tasting it because it was so darn delicious. That's when I decided that it needed a starring role in a main course. Here, the artichoke and almond salsa tops juicy, oven-seared chicken breasts. A match made in heaven? I certainly think so.

Make the artichoke-almond salsa

1. Heat the oven to 425°F.

2. Place the artichokes, grape leaves, olives, garlic, and lemon zest in a mixing bowl; add the oil, lemon juice, and salt and pepper to taste.

3. Place the almonds on a baking sheet and toast in the oven until golden, 12 minutes. Remove from the oven and finely chop the almonds. Add the almonds to the artichoke salsa. Leave the oven on for the chicken.

Make the chicken

1. Heat the oil in a large, ovenproof frying pan over medium heat. Add the chicken breasts and cook, uncovered, until light golden, 3 minutes. Turn the chicken, season with salt and pepper, and continue to cook until golden on the other side, 3 minutes. Place the pan in the oven and continue to cook until the chicken is golden and the meat is cooked through, 6 to 8 additional minutes.

2. Remove the chicken from the pan and place on a platter. Top with the artichoke-almond salsa, garnish with lemon wedges, and serve immediately.

- Wine pairing: Sauvignon Blanc
- Start with crostini topped with Gorgonzola and toasted pine nuts.
- For dessert, serve a glass of Vinsanto and biscotti.

IN THE KITCHEN peeling artichokes

Before starting, have ready a large bowl of water to which you have added the juice of 1 lemon.

Cut off the top half of an artichoke, including all of the prickly leaf points. Remove the tough outer leaves until you get to the soft light green leaves. Pare the stem to reveal the light green center.

If you're working with a large artichoke, cut it in half lengthwise, then scoop out the prickly choke in the center and discard (small artichokes don't have the choke, so there's nothing to remove).

Once you've peeled and cut the artichoke, place it in the bowl of lemon water. Follow the recipe's instructions for using artichokes.

chopped salad with chicken & ricotta salata

5 Tbs. extra-virgin olive oil

3 boneless, skinless chicken breasts (6 to 8 ounces each)

Kosher salt and freshly ground black pepper

3 Tbs. white-wine vinegar

1 small shallot, minced

½ tsp. grated lemon zest

1 small head radicchio, diced

2 small carrots, peeled and diced

2 small zucchini, cut into ½-inch dice

1 small head escarole, chopped

3 heads Belgian endive, cut into ¼-inch slices

6 ounces ricotta salata

serves 6

A CHOPPED SALAD (IT'S LITERALLY A SALAD WITH CHOPPED-UP ingredients) is a great simple dinner option. It's an easy way to make use of any raw vegetables you have hanging out in your fridge. Just chop them up and toss them with a bright lemony vinaigrette and some seared chicken, and you have a delicious, healthful meal in minutes. A few key ingredients in this recipe make the salad something special: Radicchio and Belgian endive add a touch of bitterness, while the creamy ricotta salata adds a salty, milky flavor.

I also use this recipe to share my trick for keeping chicken breasts perfectly moist. Place a small lid directly on the chicken to trap the steam and allow the chicken to retain its juices as it finishes cooking. There will be no more dry chicken coming out of your kitchen!

1. Heat 1 Tbs. of the oil in a large frying pan over medium heat. Add the chicken breasts and cook until light golden, 4 to 5 minutes. Turn the chicken, season with salt and pepper, and continue to cook with a lid that's smaller than the pan placed directly on top of the chicken until the chicken is golden and cooked through, 5 to 6 minutes. Let the chicken cool.

2. In the meantime, in a small bowl, whisk together the remaining 4 Tbs. of oil, the vinegar, shallots, and lemon zest. Season to taste with salt and pepper.

3. When the chicken has cooled, cut it into ½-inch pieces.

continued on p. 126

- Wine pairing: Sauvignon Blanc
- Make homemade roasted pita chips and serve with feta puréed with paprika, cayenne, and a spoon of yogurt to get to a thick paste consistency.
- Chocolate brownie sundaes are the perfect ending to the meal. Serve warm brownies topped with vanilla ice cream and warm chocolate sauce.

4. In a large bowl, toss together the radicchio, carrots, zucchini, escarole, and endive. Add the ricotta salata and chicken and toss with the vinaigrette.

5. Serve immediately.

IN THE KITCHEN cooking chicken breasts

I thank my cooking teacher, Madeleine Kamman, for this ingenious technique for making moist chicken breasts. Warm a frying pan over medium-high heat and add oil until it ripples (use whatever amount is called for in your recipe). Add the chicken and cook on one side until golden, 4 to 5 minutes. Turn the chicken, season with salt and pepper, and place a pan lid directly on top of the chicken. Be sure the lid is smaller than the circumference of the pan. Cook until the chicken breasts are slightly firm to the touch or the internal temperature is 175°F.

green curry chicken with thai basil

¼ tsp. ground coriander

¼ tsp. ground cloves

¼ tsp. ground cinnamon

¼ tsp. ground cardamom

Pinch of ground turmeric

4 Tbs. fish sauce or nam pla

4 cloves garlic, minced

2-inch piece fresh ginger, peeled and minced

1 tsp. ground black pepper

6 boneless, skinless chicken thighs (about 1½ pounds), cut into 1-inch pieces

1 Tbs. vegetable oil

3 Tbs. Thai green curry paste

2 cups canned unsweetened low-fat coconut milk

1 cup chicken stock

3 Tbs. light brown sugar

1 pound green beans, ends removed and cut into 1½-inch pieces

1 Tbs. freshly squeezed lime juice

1 cup fresh Thai basil sprigs

serves 6

THE ADDITION OF THAI BASIL SPRIGS, WHICH ARE SWEETER THAN Mediterranean basil and have a subtle anise flavor, enhances the classic Thai flavors of the dish. Thai basil can be found at most Asian markets, but if you can't find it, substitute Mediterranean basil (this is the basil common to supermarkets and backyard gardens) instead.

This is another great make-ahead dish. Consider doubling the recipe and placing half in a plastic container and freezing. On the morning you're going to serve the curry, simply place the container in the refrigerator. About 30 minutes before serving, place the half-frozen contents in a saucepan over low heat and warm until hot. In the meantime, you can prepare the rice.

1. Combine the coriander, cloves, cinnamon, cardamom, turmeric, 2 Tbs. of fish sauce or nam pla, the garlic, ginger, and pepper in a medium bowl. Add the chicken and stir together. Refrigerate, covered, for 1 hour.

2. Heat the oil in a deep frying pan over medium heat. Add the chicken pieces and cook, stirring, until golden on the outside, 2 to 3 minutes.

3. In a large bowl, whisk together the curry paste, coconut milk, chicken stock, brown sugar, and the remaining 2 Tbs. of fish sauce. Add this mixture and the green beans to the chicken and stir well.

4. Simmer the chicken mixture, covered, until the sauce thickens slightly and the beans and chicken are cooked, 10 to 15 minutes. Add the lime juice and basil sprigs and simmer uncovered for 5 minutes.

5. Serve immediately.

SERVING SUGGESTIONS

- Wine pairing: Off-dry Riesling
- Serve this scrumptious stew over steamed jasmine rice.
- Make a simple dessert of papaya wedges drizzled with freshly squeezed lime juice.

couscous salad with smoked chicken, dates & roasted pistachios

2 Tbs. red-wine vinegar

¼ cup balsamic vinegar

5 Tbs. extra-virgin olive oil

1 shallot, minced

Kosher salt and freshly ground black pepper

1½ cups Israeli couscous

3 smoked chicken breasts or 1 small smoked turkey breast (about 1½ pounds total), skinned and boned

½ cup pitted and halved dates, coarsely chopped

½ cup dried apricots, coarsely chopped

1 cup roasted, salted pistachios

2 Tbs. coarsely chopped fresh flat-leaf parsley

serves 6

SERVING SUGGESTIONS

- Wine pairing: Pinot Gris
- For dessert, serve coconut ice cream drizzled with warm chocolate sauce.

PREPARING COUSCOUS IS A NECESSARY KITCHEN SKILL TO MASTER for those nights when you need to get dinner on the table quickly. While cooking couscous is simple—you just add it to boiling water and allow it to steep—the key is to then turn out the cooked couscous onto a clean baking sheet and rake through it with your fingers to separate the pellets and create a light and fluffy end result.

The smoky flavor of the chicken in this salad permeates the dish, delighting your palate with a variety of flavors and textures.

1. In a large bowl, whisk together the red-wine vinegar, balsamic vinegar, olive oil, and shallots. Season with salt and pepper. Set aside.

2. Bring 2½ cups of water to a boil. Add the couscous, turn off the heat, cover with a lid, and let sit for 5 minutes.

3. After 5 minutes, dump the couscous onto a baking sheet and rake and separate the grains with your fingertips. Set aside until cool.

4. Whisk the vinaigrette together again. Cut or tear the chicken or turkey into ¾-inch pieces and combine in a large bowl with the dates, apricots, pistachios, couscous, and parsley. Add the vinaigrette and toss together. Season to taste with salt and pepper and serve immediately. The smokiness of the chicken or turkey will come through.

IN THE PANTRY couscous

Couscous is miniature wheat pasta from North Africa and the Middle East. In North Africa, it is made by rubbing durum semolina and water to make coarse granules the size of a pin head. Israeli couscous is much larger and is extruded then baked to give it a nutty flavor. Both cook in minutes. I store both in my pantry; when well sealed, they keep for 6 months.

chicken, escarole, persimmon & pomegranate salad

Kosher salt and freshly ground black pepper

3 boneless, skinless chicken breasts (6 to 8 ounces each)

1 cup late-harvest wine

1 shallot, minced

1 Tbs. white-wine vinegar

2 Tbs. white balsamic vinegar

4 Tbs. extra-virgin olive oil

½ pomegranate

1 large bunch escarole, torn into 1½ to 2-inch pieces

3 Fuju persimmons, peeled and cut into ¼-inch slices, or 3 apples or pears, thinly sliced

2 cups red seedless grapes, halved

serves 6

SERVING SUGGESTIONS

- Wine pairing: Gewürztraminer
- To start, make a simple white bean soup and top with crispy bacon.
- For dessert, grill fresh figs and serve with a wedge of Gorgonzola.

CONTRASTING FLAVORS AND TEXTURES COME TOGETHER TO CREATE this harmonious and satisfying salad. But what makes this salad most interesting is the reduced late-harvest-wine vinaigrette. It adds a sweetness that pairs beautifully with the fruit.

If you have leftover chicken, use it in this salad instead of cooking more. Be sure, though, that the chicken you use hasn't been cooked with intense spices or flavoring, as that will detract from the flavor combination of this dish.

1. Bring a large saucepan of salted water to a boil. Add the chicken breasts, cover, and simmer until firm to the touch and cooked through, 10 to 12 minutes. Remove from the pan and set aside on a plate to cool. When the chicken is cool, shred it into ½-inch strips and set aside. (I find it easiest to shred the chicken by holding one breast with my hand and using a fork to pull strips and shred the meat with the other hand.)

2. Place the wine in a saucepan and bring to a boil over medium-high heat. Simmer until reduced to about 4 Tbs. Watch this closely—you don't want the wine to reduce too far down where it's no longer liquidy. When the wine has reduced, add the shallots, white-wine vinegar, balsamic vinegar, and oil. Whisk together and season with salt and pepper.

3. Fill a bowl with cold water. Remove the seeds from the pomegranate by submerging the pomegranate in the water and rubbing your hands over the skin and white membrane to remove it. The skin and membrane should float to the top, and the seeds will fall to the bottom of the bowl. Discard the skin and membrane. Scoop the seeds from the water and place on paper towels to dry. Reserve.

4. Place the chicken, pomegranates seeds, escarole, persimmon slices, grapes, and vinaigrette in a large bowl. Toss together and serve immediately.

crispy chicken & potatoes with mustard, rosemary & capers

2 Tbs. unsalted butter, at room temperature

3 Tbs. grainy mustard

1 Tbs. chopped fresh rosemary

1 Tbs. chopped capers

1 whole chicken (about 4 pounds), quartered

3 Tbs. olive oil

Kosher salt and freshly ground black pepper

1½ pounds roasting potatoes, cut into 1½-inch chunks

serves 4

THERE IS SOMETHING SO COMFORTING ABOUT THE AROMA OF chicken roasting in the oven. Few dinners are simpler to make and have the ability to satisfy quite like a crispy-skinned, succulent roasted chicken. In this version, compound butter with grainy mustard, rosemary, and capers is slathered under the bird's skin. As the chicken perches on a bed of potatoes while roasting, the butter melts, simultaneously seasoning the chicken and bathing the potatoes in flavor. Any combination of aromatics, herbs, and spices can be used in the compound butter, making this one-pan meal virtually limitless in its variations.

1. Heat the oven to 400°F. In a small bowl, combine the butter, mustard, rosemary, and capers.

2. Loosen the skin of the chicken by gently sliding your fingers between the skin and the meat. Rub the mustard-herb mixture beneath the skin. Coat the outside of the chicken with 1 Tbs. of oil and season with salt and pepper.

3. Wash and dry the potatoes. Place them in a single layer in a roasting pan. Drizzle with the remaining 2 Tbs. of olive oil and season generously with salt and pepper. Place the chicken pieces on top of the potatoes and roast uncovered in the middle of the oven for 50 to 60 minutes. Remove the chicken from the pan (be sure all the mustard butter drips off the chicken and stays in the roasting pan) and temporarily set it on a platter.

- Wine pairing: Chardonnay
- Start with watercress and apple salad with toasted pistachios.
- Serve mint chocolate chip ice cream with chocolate wafers for dessert.

Toss the potatoes. Place the chicken back on top of the potatoes and continue to roast the chicken until the thickest part registers 165°F on an instant-read meat thermometer, 20 to 30 minutes. Let the chicken rest, covered loosely with foil, for 10 minutes.

4. Cut each breast into 2 pieces across the breast. Cut the legs into 2 thighs and 2 drumsticks. Transfer the chicken to a platter and serve alongside the potatoes.

AT THE MARKET potatoes

Russet or baking potatoes have a lot of starch and are best for mashed potatoes, French fries, and gnocchi, as well as for baking. Red potatoes, Yellow Finn, and Yukon Gold potatoes are good for steaming and for soups, stews, potato salads, and dishes where you need the potato to hold its shape.

spice-dusted chicken skewers with harissa yogurt sauce

12 bamboo skewers, about 5 to 6 inches long

1½ tsp. whole cumin seeds

1 whole cardamom pod

1½ tsp. crushed whole coriander seeds

1½ tsp. whole fennel seeds

3 whole black peppercorns

Kosher salt and freshly ground black pepper

1¾ pounds boneless chicken breasts, cut into ¾-inch pieces

2 Tbs. extra-virgin olive oil

1¼ cups Greek yogurt

1½ Tbs. freshly grated ginger

1 to 2 tsp. harissa paste

serves 6

BONELESS, SKINLESS CHICKEN BREAST SOMETIMES GETS A BAD RAP for being bland and dry. That is certainly not the case in this dish. Dusted with cumin, cardamom, coriander, fennel, and black pepper, these grilled chicken skewers are anything but ordinary. Toasting the whole spices in a pan and grinding them just before use brings all of their nuanced flavors to life. With a zesty fresh ginger and harissa yogurt sauce served alongside, this meal really is a party in your mouth.

1. Soak the bamboo skewers in water for 20 minutes.

2. In the meantime, place the cumin, cardamom, coriander, and fennel seeds in a dry frying pan over medium-high heat and shake the pan until aromatic, 30 to 60 seconds. In a spice grinder, grind the peppercorns until coarsely ground. Add the toasted spices and pulse until crushed but not a fine dust. Add ½ tsp. salt. Place the spice mixture on a dinner plate and shake the plate to distribute evenly.

3. Remove the skewers from the water and thread the chicken on the skewers, distributing the chicken evenly. Brush the chicken with 1 Tbs. of oil. Dip the skewered chicken into the spice mixture to coat heavily.

4. Heat an outdoor grill and set the grate at 4 to 5 inches from the heat source. Alternately, you can cook the skewers indoors by heating a nonstick, ridged grill pan over medium-high heat for 10 minutes.

5. While the grill is heating, combine the yogurt, ginger, harissa, and the remaining 1 Tbs. oil. Season with salt and pepper.

- Wine pairing: Tempranillo
- Start with a tomato salad with preserved lemon and a cumin vinaigrette.
- For dessert, serve lemon frozen yogurt topped with a fresh orange compote and sprinkled with toasted sliced almonds.

6. Grill the chicken skewers, turning occasionally, until the chicken is done, 8 to 10 minutes.

7. To serve, place the skewers on a platter and serve the ginger yogurt alongside in a small bowl.

IN THE PANTRY greek yogurt

Greek yogurt is much thicker than regular yogurt, and it's great to have on hand. I use it for many different things: as a simple sauce for meat and fish, as a garnish for soups, and as a topping on a baked potato. It's also great when mixed with honey and drizzled over fresh fruit for dessert, when mixed into smoothies, and as breakfast with berries. The flavor is delicious and though it's thicker, it's not any more caloric than the regular type.

lemon turkey cutlets

1¾ pounds turkey breast, skin and bone removed

1 cup unbleached all-purpose flour

Kosher salt and freshly ground black pepper

3 eggs

1½ cups panko

1 Tbs. chopped fresh oregano

1 Tbs. grated lemon zest

1 cup grated Grana Padano

2 Tbs. olive oil

2 Tbs. unsalted butter

Orange and lemon wedges, for garnish

serves 6

THIS IS THE PERFECT DINNER TO TURN TO WHEN YOU'RE PRESSED for time. By pounding the turkey breasts into thin cutlets, you cut cooking time dramatically and ensure the meat cooks evenly and remains moist. Coated in panko (breadcrumbs that are larger and airier than traditional breadcrumbs) that's been seasoned with fresh oregano, lemon zest, and Grana Padano cheese, these turkey cutlets are crisp and flavorful, perfect with a salad, rice, or lightly sautéed vegetables. Don't forget to serve with lots of orange and lemon wedges; squeezing fresh juice over the warm cutlets makes them irresistible.

1. Cut each turkey breast on the bias and on the diagonal into ¾-inch-thick slices. Place each piece between two pieces of waxed paper or plastic wrap. With a large flat meat pounder, pound the turkey until it is ¼ to ⅜ inch thick.

2. Have ready a baking sheet covered with foil. Place the flour in a bowl and season with salt and pepper. Crack the eggs into a small bowl and season with salt and pepper; whisk well. Combine the panko, oregano, lemon zest, Grana Padano, salt, and pepper in a third bowl. To bread the turkey, dip both sides of the turkey in the flour, shaking off the excess. Next, dip the turkey in the egg mixture, letting the excess drain. Dip the turkey in the breadcrumb mixture and use your fingers to coat each side with breadcrumbs. Tap off the excess. Set aside in a single layer on the baking sheet. Refrigerate until ready to use.

- Wine pairing: Viognier

- These cutlets are especially good with a lightly dressed arugula and orange salad served right on top.

- For dessert, serve port, a wedge of Cheddar, a few toasted walnuts, and sliced apples.

3. In a large frying pan over medium-high heat, warm the oil and melt the butter. Add the turkey in a single layer. Do not overcrowd the pan, so cook in batches if necessary. Cook the turkey, turning occasionally, until the pieces are golden brown on each side, 8 to 10 minutes total.

4. To serve, place the turkey on a platter and serve immediately, garnished with orange and lemon wedges.

IN THE KITCHEN pounding turkey breasts

Pounding turkey or chicken breasts ensures evenness in cooking. With the breast between two sheets of plastic wrap and working on a sturdy work surface, use a flat meat pounder, a mallet, or even the bottom of a sturdy frying pan to pound the breast to the thickness called for in your recipe.

warm moroccan chicken & sweet potato salad

FOR THE CHICKEN

3 bone-in, skin-on chicken breasts (1½ to 2 pounds total)

1 tsp. mild curry powder

1 tsp. ground cumin

½ tsp. kosher salt

FOR THE SALAD

2 tsp. mild curry powder

1 Tbs. ground cumin

Kosher salt

7 Tbs. extra-virgin olive oil

1½ pounds sweet potatoes, peeled and cut into ¾-inch dice (about 3 cups)

¼ cup whole almonds with skin, coarsely chopped

⅓ cup pumpkin seeds

1½ Tbs. cumin seeds

¼ cup red-wine vinegar

1 large clove garlic, minced

1 large tomato, peeled, seeded, and diced

4 green onions, white and green parts, thinly sliced

½ cup chopped fresh cilantro stems, plus 3 cups fresh cilantro leaves

serves 6

THIS POTATO SALAD IS LIKE NO POTATO SALAD YOU'VE EVER TASTED.
Each component is delicious in its own right, so combining them makes a show-stopping dish. Like most Moroccan recipes, this one features a variety of aromatic spices, so your taste buds are in for an exotic treat. While the salad is a nice weeknight meal, it also is perfect when entertaining if you cook the chicken ahead of time and reheat it before combining all the ingredients.

Thanks to my South Australian chef friend, Mark McNamara, for his inspiration.

Cook the chicken

1. Remove the skin from the chicken and discard. Place the chicken in a large saucepan with the curry powder, cumin, and salt. Cover with water and bring to a boil over high heat. Reduce the heat to low and simmer until the chicken is tender, 20 minutes. Remove from the pan and discard the liquid. Let the chicken cool.

2. When the chicken is cool, remove the meat from the bone and tear into pieces. Set aside.

Make the salad

1. Heat the oven to 375°F.

2. Mix the curry powder, cumin, and 1½ tsp. salt. Toss half of the spice mixture with 1 Tbs. of oil and the sweet potatoes. Spread in a baking pan and roast until tender, 30 minutes.

3. Toss the almonds and pumpkin seeds with the remaining spice mixture and 1 Tbs. of oil, place on a baking sheet, and toast in the oven until the almonds and pumpkins seeds are golden, 10 to 12 minutes. Set aside.

continued on p. 138

- Wine pairing: Gewürztraminer or dry rosé
- To start, serve pita chips with spicy carrot dip scented with cumin, cayenne, and ginger.
- For dessert, serve ginger cookies with mint tea.

4. For the dressing, place the cumin seeds in a dry frying pan over medium-high heat and toss until they are aromatic and begin to crackle, 30 to 40 seconds. Remove from the heat and place in a small bowl. Add the vinegar, garlic, and remaining 5 Tbs. of oil.

5. When the potatoes are done, add the chicken pieces, almonds, pumpkin seeds, tomatoes, green onions, chopped cilantro, and half of the dressing; mix well. Place the salad in the center of a serving plate. Drizzle the remaining dressing around the plate and scatter with cilantro leaves.

IN THE KITCHEN poaching chicken

Poaching chicken—simply placing chicken in a pan of water and cooking until tender—is an easy technique that gives you two results in one. You get not only succulent, juicy meat but also delicious flavorful stock. Before poaching, remove any skin from the chicken so that you won't have as much fat to skim from the finished broth. Vary the ingredients you cook with the chicken to get different-flavored broth. Your options are only limited by your imagination.

rigatoni with chicken, tomatoes & cream

2 Tbs. extra-virgin olive oil

2 pounds boneless, skinless chicken thighs, fat removed, cut into 1-inch pieces

1 small red onion, diced

2 cloves garlic, minced

Pinch of crushed red pepper flakes

2 bay leaves

1 tsp. chopped fresh sage

1 tsp. chopped fresh rosemary

1 cup dry red wine, such as Chianti or Cabernet Sauvignon

One 28-ounce can imported Italian tomatoes, chopped

1 cup heavy cream

1 cup grated Parmigiano-Reggiano

Kosher salt and freshly ground black pepper

1 pound dried 100% semolina rigatoni

serves 6

SERVING SUGGESTIONS

- Wine pairing: Sangiovese
- As a starter, serve a butter lettuce salad with garlic croutons.
- For dessert, slice Comice or Bartlett pears and serve with Italian Teleme.

PASTA IS OFTEN MY GO-TO STAPLE WHEN I'M PRESSED FOR TIME OR making dinner at the last minute. This is one of those dishes that I threw together using items I always have on hand in my pantry; it was so delicious and comforting that I now turn to it again and again.

The oil from the sautéed chicken thighs serves as the perfect base for a homemade tomato sauce that is enhanced with onions, garlic, fresh herbs, and red wine. But my favorite part of preparing this dish is stirring in the cream. The white cream looks like a satin ribbon as it swirls into the deep red sauce, ultimately creating a vibrant, salmon-hued sauce. One taste of this simple sauce tossed with rigatoni and you'll never turn to store-bought sauce again.

1. Heat the oil in a large frying pan over medium-high heat. Add the chicken and cook, turning occasionally, until golden on all sides, 6 to 8 minutes. Remove the chicken from the pan and set aside.

2. Reduce the heat to medium and add the onions, garlic, red pepper flakes, bay leaves, sage, and rosemary. Cook, stirring occasionally, until the onions are golden brown, 10 to 15 minutes. Turn the heat to high, add the wine, and boil until the wine evaporates, 3 to 5 minutes. Add the browned chicken pieces and tomatoes and bring to a boil. Reduce the heat to low and simmer, covered, until the sauce thickens, 30 minutes. Remove the bay leaves and discard. Add the cream and half of the Parmigiano-Reggiano and stir together. Season to taste with salt and pepper.

3. Bring a large pot of salted water to a boil. Add the rigatoni and cook until al dente, 10 to 12 minutes, or according to the package directions. Drain the pasta, put it back in the pan, and toss with the tomato sauce. Place on a platter, sprinkle with the remaining Parmigiano-Reggiano, and serve immediately.

"oven-fried" chicken legs

1½ cups dried homemade breadcrumbs

Kosher salt and freshly ground black pepper

¼ tsp. dried thyme

½ tsp. paprika

1 cup Lime Aïoli (recipe on p. 142)

6 whole chicken legs (2½ to 3 pounds total)

serves 6

SERVING SUGGESTIONS

• **Wine pairing: Pinot Noir**

• **Serve with buttermilk mashed potatoes and buttered green beans.**

I LOVE FRIED CHICKEN AS MUCH AS THE NEXT GIRL, BUT IT'S NOT something I eat on a regular basis for obvious health reasons. This baked version is just as tasty (I actually would argue that it's even more delicious) and far less artery clogging. Coating the chicken legs in homemade aïoli (or even a mock version using store-bought mayonnaise and a touch of garlic) before breading them adds an additional, unique layer of flavor. Varying the type of aïoli—from lime to lemon caper to tomato and hot pepper—changes the flavor profile of the chicken entirely. Master this one recipe and you'll have countless new meals to enjoy.

1. Heat the oven to 350°F.

2. Place the breadcrumbs, 1 tsp. salt, 1 tsp. pepper, thyme, and paprika in a large bowl.

3. Place the lime aïoli in a bowl with the chicken legs and toss to coat. Place the chicken in the bowl with the breadcrumb mixture and coat well. Place the chicken on a lightly greased baking sheet and bake until the juices run clear, about 45 minutes. Remove from the oven and serve immediately.

continued on p. 142

lime aïoli

1 egg yolk

1 tsp. Dijon mustard

½ cup extra-virgin olive oil

½ cup vegetable, canola, corn, or safflower oil

2 to 3 cloves garlic, minced

Freshly squeezed lime juice, to taste

Kosher salt

makes about 1 cup

Add the yolk and mustard to a small bowl. Combine the olive oil and unflavored oil in a liquid measuring cup. Add 1 Tbs. of the combined oils to the yolk and mustard and whisk together until an emulsion is formed. Drop by drop, add the remaining oil to the emulsion, whisking constantly. Continue to do this, drop by drop, in a steady stream, whisking, until all of the oil has been added. Do not add the oil too quickly, and be sure that the emulsion is homogeneous before adding more oil. Season with garlic, lime juice, and salt.

IN THE KITCHEN tips when making aïoli

- Make sure all ingredients are at room temperature.

- Add the oil drop by drop, whisking constantly, until an emulsion is formed. You must work slowly.

- Do not add more oil until the last drops of oil are emulsified.

- For each egg yolk, you can emulsify 1 cup of oil.

frying-pan-roasted chicken with caramelized oranges & lemons

Kosher salt and freshly ground black pepper

One 3½- to 4-pound chicken

2 Tbs. unsalted butter

4 paper-thin slices seedless orange

4 paper-thin slices lemon, seeds removed

1 Tbs. canola oil

Orange and lemon wedges, for garnish

serves 4 to 6

THIS FRYING-PAN-ROASTED CHICKEN IS QUITE POSSIBLY THE MOST succulent chicken you'll ever eat. Submerging the bird in a simple brine made of water and salt for 24 hours causes the chicken to soak up the seasoned water, ensuring especially moist, tender, flavorful meat. But that's not all. Caramelized slices of citrus slipped beneath the skin add a layer of sweet, fresh flavor and are visually stunning peeking through the chicken's crispy exterior. Also, because the chicken is butterflied, it roasts much faster than a chicken kept completely whole. Talk about a win-win-win!

1. To make the brining solution, place 8 cups of water and ½ cup salt in a bowl. Stir to dissolve. Add the chicken and press down to submerge it in the water completely. If the bird isn't completely submerged, add additional water and salt to the ratio of 1 cup water to 2 Tbs. salt until completely submerged. You can weight the bird with a small plate and a heavy can. Cover and place in the refrigerator for 24 hours.

2. Melt the butter in a large, nonstick frying pan over medium-high heat. Add the orange and lemon slices in a single layer and cook, turning occasionally, until soft and light golden, 5 to 8 minutes.

3. Remove the chicken from the brining solution and pat dry with paper towels inside and out. Cut the chicken down the back, removing the backbone. (You can also have your butcher do this.)

4. Turn the chicken over and place it on the work surface skin side up. Press on the chicken gently so it lays flat. Using your fingers and working carefully not to tear the skin, separate the skin from the breast and thigh. Working with one slice of lemon or orange at a time, insert the fruit in a single layer between the skin and the flesh of the chicken, distributing evenly. They should cover the breast and thigh of the chicken. Season the chicken on both sides with salt and pepper.

continued on p. 145

- Wine pairing: Viognier
- For a side dish, serve steamed basmati rice scented with a few strips of orange and lemon peel. Alongside, serve an endive, fennel, radicchio, and arugula salad with toasted pine nuts, orange segments, and golden raisins.

5. Heat the oven to 450°F.

6. Warm the oil in a large, heavy, ovenproof frying pan over high heat until the oil is rippling. Place the chicken in the pan, skin side down, and immediately transfer the pan to the oven and roast for 10 minutes. Turn the chicken and continue to roast until the juices of the thigh run clear when a skewer is inserted and an instant-read thermometer registers 175°F when inserted into the thickest part of the flesh, 30 to 35 minutes. Baste with juices from the pan halfway through the roasting.

7. To serve, cut the chicken into serving-size pieces and place on a platter. Garnish with orange and lemon wedges.

IN THE KITCHEN butterflying a chicken

Although you can ask your butcher to butterfly a chicken for you, this is a technique you should master.

Be sure the chicken is dry (so that it's not too slippery) and hold it firmly in one hand while using a large chef's knife to cut halfway down one side of the backbone.

Again, holding the chicken firmly, use the knife to slice halfway down the bird on the other side of the backbone. Discard the backbone.

With the bird laying inside down on the work surface, use both hands to press down, flattening the chicken.

roasted game hens with prosciutto & mushrooms

6 Cornish game hens, about 1½ pounds each

Kosher salt and freshly ground black pepper

3 Tbs. unsalted butter

¾ pound wild mushrooms, such as chanterelles, morels, and porcinis, finely chopped

1½ tsp. chopped fresh thyme

Three 1/16-inch-thick slices prosciutto (3 to 4 ounces), diced

serves 6

THE TERM "GAME HEN" IS A BIT MISLEADING SINCE THESE ANIMALS are not actually hunted. They are young chickens, generally about 1½ pounds each, raised to be meaty and slightly lighter in flavor than traditional chicken. Game hens are perfect for roasting and make for an incredibly elegant meal, with each guest receiving his or her very own bird. In this version, a sauté of finely chopped mushrooms and prosciutto is gently rubbed under the skin. The game hens are then brushed with butter and roasted until golden and crisp.

1. Remove the neck and giblets from the game hens, rinse with cold water, and pat dry inside and out. Set the neck and giblets aside. Sprinkle the inside of the hens with salt and pepper.

2. Melt 1 Tbs. of butter in a large frying pan over medium heat. Add the mushrooms, season with salt and pepper, add the thyme, and cook, stirring occasionally, until the mushrooms are soft and the mixture is dry, 3 to 5 minutes. Remove the mushrooms from the pan, place in a bowl, and let cool. Add the prosciutto to the mushrooms and stir the stuffing until mixed.

3. Working with one hen at a time, insert your fingertips at the wing end of the breast and gently loosen the skin over the breast and around the thigh and drumstick. Be careful not to tear the skin off the game hens. Divide the stuffing evenly into six portions. Place one portion of stuffing under the skin of one game hen with your fingers, distributing it evenly over the breast and thigh of the hens. With kitchen string, tie the legs together at the ankle. Repeat for the remaining hens.

- Wine pairing: Pinot Noir
- Serve these two side dishes for the game hens: quinoa pilaf and wilted spinach.

4. Heat the oven to 400°F. Arrange the birds breast side up on a rack set in a shallow roasting pan. Melt the remaining 2 Tbs. butter and brush the skin with half of the butter. Sprinkle with salt and pepper. Place the game hens in the oven and roast for 20 minutes. Remove from the oven, brush with the remaining melted butter, and then continue to roast until the juices run clear from the thickest part of the thigh and an instant-read thermometer registers 170°F, 25 to 30 minutes. Remove the game hens to a platter and let stand for 10 minutes before serving.

5. To serve, place one game hen on each plate.

IN THE KITCHEN trussing a game hen

Trussing a game hen or chicken helps the bird to have a good shape and cook more evenly. There are several ways to do it, but I always go for the simplest technique: Tuck the wing tips back and underneath the hen or chicken. With a piece of cotton kitchen string, tie the two legs together at the ankle.

5

BEYOND

fish STICKS

THE RECIPES

TECHNIQUES MADE SIMPLE

clams with chorizo & orange

4 Tbs. extra-virgin olive oil

½ pound fresh chorizo, removed from the casings and crumbled

2 cloves garlic, thinly sliced

1 tomato, peeled, seeded, and chopped (fresh or canned)

One 2-inch piece orange peel, white pith removed

1 cup dry white wine, such as Sauvignon Blanc

3 pounds fresh Manila clams, or other small clams, scrubbed

Kosher salt and freshly ground black pepper

1 Calabrian pepper, minced, or a pinch of crushed red pepper flakes

2 Tbs. chopped fresh flat-leaf parsley

serves 6

SERVING SUGGESTIONS

• Wine pairing: Albariño

• Start the meal with bruschetta topped with mixed greens and strips of prosciutto or jamon serrano.

• For dessert, serve vanilla bean ice cream with a blueberry maple syrup compote.

CHORIZO IS SPANISH PORK SAUSAGE THAT GETS ITS DISTINCT RED HUE from smoked paprika, or pimentón. It can be either spicy or sweet, depending on which type of pimentón is used. In this dish, the smoky sausage serves as the perfect foil to the briny sweet Manila clams. The addition of orange peel to the white wine and tomato stock adds subtle citrusy notes and serves to enhance all of the flavors in this complex and delicious dish.

1. Warm the oil in a large frying pan over medium heat. Add the chorizo and cook, stirring occasionally, until cooked through, 4 minutes. Remove the chorizo and reserve in a bowl. Drain off and discard all but 2 Tbs. of the fat in the pan.

2. Add the garlic to the pan and cook for 1 minute. Increase the heat to high, add the tomatoes, orange peel, and white wine, and simmer until reduced by half, 2 minutes. Add the clams, cover, and cook until the clams open, 4 to 5 minutes. (If any clams do not open, discard them.) Season with salt and pepper. Add the chorizo, Calabrian peppers or red pepper flakes, and chopped parsley and toss together.

3. Before serving, remove the orange peel and discard. Ladle the clams and chorizo into bowls and spoon some of the juices over the clams. Serve immediately.

IN THE PANTRY pimentón

Pimentón is smoked paprika used in Spain to make chorizo and to flavor paella. There are 3 types—sweet, or dulce; medium; and hot, or picante. I keep all three kinds on hand in my kitchen and use them according to how much heat I want to add to a dish. The varying levels of heat depend upon the particular chiles used. Sweet is mild in flavor and light orange in color while medium is just slightly hot. Hot is made with several different types of pepper and is spicy hot. Use all of them sparingly; a little goes a long way.

fettucine with shrimp, tomatoes & pancetta

1 pound dry fettuccine

3 Tbs. extra-virgin olive oil

2 Tbs. unsalted butter

2 ounces pancetta, diced

2 cloves garlic, very thinly sliced

1¼ pounds large shrimp (31 to 35 per pound), peeled, deveined, and butterflied

6 plum tomatoes (about 1 pound), peeled, seeded, and cut into wedges

Large pinch of crushed red pepper flakes

½ cup Kalamata olives, pitted

1 tsp. finely grated orange zest

½ cup freshly squeezed orange juice

⅓ cup ouzo or Pernod®

Kosher salt and freshly ground black pepper

2 Tbs. chopped fresh flat-leaf parsley

serves 6

THIS PASTA DISH IS WONDERFULLY UNCOMPLICATED IN ITS PREPARATION. My advice is to get all of your ingredients ready to go before you bring the pasta water to a boil. This is called *mise en place*—or set in place—in chef lingo. Then you can prepare the shrimp and simple sauce in the short time it takes for the fettuccine to cook. Be sure to taste before serving. You might need another dash of the anise-flavored ouzo to really make this dish sing!

1. Bring a pot of salted water to a boil. Add the pasta and simmer until al dente, 8 to 12 minutes, or according to the package directions. Drain and set aside.

2. Heat a large frying pan over medium-high heat. Add the oil and butter, then add the pancetta and cook until light golden, about 5 minutes. Add the garlic and cook for 1 minute. Add the shrimp and cook, stirring and shaking the pan constantly, until the shrimp are pink, 3 minutes. With a slotted spoon, remove the shrimp and place in a bowl.

3. Add the tomatoes, crushed red pepper flakes, olives, orange zest, and orange juice, and cook over medium-high heat, stirring occasionally, for 2 to 3 minutes. Add the ouzo or Pernod and simmer, stirring, for 1 minute. Season with salt and pepper to taste.

4. Toss the cooked pasta with the shrimp, parsley, and sauce. Serve immediately.

SERVING SUGGESTIONS

• Wine pairing: Un-oaked Chardonnay

• Serve with an arugula salad with shaved Parmigiano-Reggiano and lemon olive oil.

• Finish the meal with peach crisp topped with vanilla ice cream.

cod braised with leeks, potatoes & thyme

1½ cups chicken stock or bottled clam juice

2 tsp. Dijon mustard

2 Tbs. capers, drained

3 sprigs fresh thyme

½ cup dry white wine, such as Sauvignon Blanc

1 pound Yukon Gold potatoes, peeled and thinly sliced

2 leeks, white and 1 inch of the green parts, thinly sliced

Kosher salt and freshly ground black pepper

1½ pounds cod fillets, cut into 6 serving pieces

1 tsp. freshly squeezed lemon juice

1 tsp. freshly grated lemon zest

Fresh flat-leaf parsley sprigs, for garnish

Lemon wedges, for garnish

serves 6

THIS ONE-POT DISH WAS BORN OF NECESSITY ON ONE OF THOSE nights where all of a sudden it's dinnertime and I realize I haven't given dinner a single thought all day. On this occasion, I scoured the contents of my refrigerator and married some leeks, potatoes, and thyme in a pot with chicken stock and white wine. I added cod fillets, which turned out perfectly flaky. Just like that, a simple and scrumptious new dish was created.

1. In a large frying pan over medium-high heat, bring the chicken stock or clam juice to a boil. Reduce the heat to maintain a simmer. Add the mustard, capers, thyme, and wine and whisk gently. Place a layer of potatoes in the pan and top with a layer of leeks. Sprinkle with salt and pepper. Cover the pan and cook until the potatoes and leeks are tender, 12 minutes.

2. Remove the cover from the pan and place the cod fillets on top of the leeks. Sprinkle the lemon juice and lemon zest over the fish and season with salt and pepper. Cover and cook until the fish is flaky, 5 to 6 minutes. Remove the cover. Push the fish and potatoes aside and remove and discard the thyme sprigs.

3. Ladle the vegetables and fish into wide soup bowls and garnish with chopped parsley and lemon wedges. Serve immediately.

SERVING SUGGESTIONS

- Wine pairing: Cava
- Start with a citrus salad with red onions and mint.

- With the main course, serve thin slices of toasted focaccia drizzled with extra-virgin olive oil scented with lemon and a sprinkle of Maldon salt.

fried brown rice with crab & peas

1½ cups brown rice

Kosher salt

1½ cups shelled English peas, fresh or frozen

2 Tbs. peanut oil

1 Tbs. freshly grated ginger

1½ cups picked fresh crabmeat

1 Tbs. rice vinegar

1 Tbs. soy sauce; more as needed

2 cups fresh pea shoots

serves 6

I DON'T KNOW ANYONE WHO DOESN'T LOVE FRIED RICE. WITH THIS homemade version, fried rice no longer has to be a guilty pleasure when ordering cheap Chinese take-out. This dish is filled with the crisp, clean flavors of English peas, grated ginger, and crabmeat and topped with juicy, tender fresh pea shoots. Talk about refreshing.

Although brown rice does take a bit to prepare, my trick is to always make an extralarge batch whenever I'm cooking it. After it cools, the brown rice can be stored in the freezer, making this dish not just tastier than take-out, but faster, too!

1. Place the rice in a strainer and rinse under cold water for 30 seconds.

2. Bring a large pot with 8 cups of water to a boil over high heat. Add the rice and return to a boil. Reduce the heat to medium and boil, uncovered, for 30 minutes. Drain and place the rice back in the pot off the heat. Cover with a tight-fitting lid and set aside for 10 minutes. After 10 minutes, remove the cover. Add salt to taste. Dump the rice onto a baking sheet and let cool completely in the refrigerator for at least 1 hour.

3. Bring a medium pot of water to a boil. Add the peas and simmer for 1 minute. Drain immediately.

4. Heat the oil in a large nonstick pan or wok over high heat until rippling. Add the ginger; when you can smell it, immediately add the rice and cook for 5 minutes, stirring frequently. Add the crabmeat, vinegar, soy sauce, and peas and cook, stirring, for 1 minute. Taste and season with additional soy sauce.

5. Place the rice in a large serving bowl and top with the pea shoots. Serve immediately.

- Wine pairing: Sauvignon Blanc

- Start with a salad of napa cabbage and carrots topped with peanuts, jalapeños, and cilantro and a dressing made with rice vinegar, oyster sauce, and sesame and peanut oils.

- For dessert, try fresh pineapple segments drizzled with honey and sprinkled with five-spice powder.

IN THE PANTRY the asian pantry

I love the flavors of Asian food, so I keep a number of items on hand. Here are my favorites:

- sesame oil
- chile oil
- fish sauce
- soy sauce
- tamari
- hoisin sauce
- oyster sauce
- rice vinegar

- black vinegar
- low-sodium chicken stock
- coconut milk
- five-spice powder
- Sichuan peppercorns
- star anise
- ground ginger

- garlic
- Sriracha
- ponzu
- lemongrass
- basmati and jasmine rices
- soba noodles

mussels steamed with mustard greens, lemongrass & ginger

3 pounds very fresh mussels

1 cup dry white wine, such as Sauvignon Blanc

2 Tbs. soy sauce

4 slices fresh ginger

1 stalk lemongrass, thinly sliced

6 Sichuan peppercorns

2 cups mustard greens, leaves coarsely chopped and ribs removed and discarded

Grilled Bread with Ginger Aïoli (recipe on the facing page)

serves 6

SERVING SUGGESTIONS

• Wine pairing: Dry Riesling

• Finish the meal with fresh mango and papaya drizzled with honey and sprinkled with a tiny pinch of fleur de sel.

WHEN IT COMES TO MUSSELS, FRESHNESS IS KEY, SO ASK YOUR LOCAL fishmonger to special-order them for you, if possible. They should smell and taste subtly "of the sea" and have a beautifully tender texture. In this recipe, the mussels are steamed in a white-wine stock full of Asian flavors: soy sauce, ginger, lemongrass, and Sichuan peppercorn, while mustard greens add just the right hint of heat.

1. Wash the mussels well and remove the beards. Set aside in the refrigerator.

2. In a large, heavy saucepan, heat the wine and soy sauce over high heat. Add the ginger, lemongrass, and peppercorns and simmer, uncovered, for 5 minutes. Add the mustard greens and mussels, toss together, and cook until the mussels open, 3 to 5 minutes.

3. Discard any mussels that haven't opened. To serve, spoon the mussels, mustard greens, and stock into bowls and serve with the Grilled Bread with Ginger Aïoli.

IN THE KITCHEN steaming mussels

To steam mussels, add the mussels to a pan with ½ cup water or dry white wine, such as Sauvignon Blanc. Set the pan over high heat and cover. Shake the pan periodically. Remove the lid and set aside. With tongs, remove the mussels as they open and place in a bowl. Cover the pan again and continue to cook until all of the mussels have opened removing the opened ones as you go. If any mussels do not open, discard them.

grilled bread with ginger aïoli

1 egg yolk

1 tsp. Dijon mustard

½ cup olive oil

½ cup peanut, vegetable, corn, or safflower oil

1 tsp. sesame oil

3 cloves garlic, minced

2 tsp. freshly grated ginger

1 Tbs. rice vinegar

Kosher salt and freshly ground black pepper

6 slices coarse-textured bread

makes 1 cup ginger aïoli; serves 6

1. In a small bowl, whisk the yolk, mustard, and 1 Tbs. olive oil together until an emulsion is formed. In another bowl, combine the remaining olive oil, the peanut oil, and sesame oil. Drop by drop, add the oil to the emulsion, whisking constantly. Continue to do this, drop by drop, in a steady stream, whisking, until all of the oil has been added. Do not add the oil too quickly and be sure that the emulsion is homogeneous before adding more oil.

2. Add the garlic, ginger, vinegar, and salt and pepper to taste. Thin the aïoli slightly by adding 2 Tbs. water while whisking constantly.

3. Grill, toast, or broil the bread until light golden. Top with a dollop of the aïoli.

prosciutto-wrapped halibut

2 pounds fresh halibut, preferably wild, cut across into 6 long, thin pieces

Kosher salt and freshly ground black pepper

12 slices thinly sliced prosciutto (about 3 ounces)

1 Tbs. extra-virgin olive oil

Lemon wedges, for garnish

serves 6

SERVING SUGGESTIONS

• Wine pairing: Dry rosé
• Serve with Spiced Lentils (recipe on the facing page) and a lemony fresh Herb Salad (recipe on p. 160).

THIS ELEGANT YET SIMPLE DISH IS JUST THE THING WHEN YOU WANT to pull out all the stops and do something that's simply over the top. Delicate white-fleshed halibut is wrapped in paper-thin prosciutto and then seared. The slightly sweet and salty cured meat keeps the fish incredibly moist and also imparts complex flavor. Substitute cod if your fish market doesn't have fresh halibut.

1. Heat the oven to 400°F.

2. Season the fish with salt and pepper. Lay two pieces of prosciutto slightly overlapping on the work surface and lay one piece of fish across the slices at one end of the prosciutto. Roll up the fish in the prosciutto. Repeat with the remaining fish and prosciutto.

3. Warm the oil in a large, ovenproof frying pan over medium-high heat. Add the fish and cook until the prosciutto is golden on one side. Turn the fish (be careful that the prosciutto doesn't come unwrapped) and cook on the second side until the prosciutto is golden. Immediately place the pan in the oven and continue to cook until a knife can be inserted easily into the fish, 6 to 8 minutes. Serve immediately on top of the warm lentils, with lemon wedges on the side.

AT THE MARKET prosciutto

Not all prosciutto is created equal. At the market, you will see prosciutto produced in Italy and domestically. If you want the authentic flavor of prosciutto, choose a type from Italy, either prosciutto di Parma or prosciutto di San Daniele. They will cost more than the domestic brands, but you'll get better flavor.

spiced lentils

1¼ cups French du Puy lentils

8 whole cloves, tied in a piece of cheesecloth

3 Tbs. extra-virgin olive oil

1 small red onion, minced

3 cloves garlic, minced

Pinch crushed red pepper flakes

1 cup tomatoes, peeled, seeded, and chopped (fresh or canned)

1½ cups fish stock or bottled clam juice

¼ cup chopped fresh flat-leaf parsley

2 tsp. chopped fresh oregano

1 to 2 Tbs. freshly squeezed lemon juice

Kosher salt and freshly ground black pepper

serves 6

1. Sort the lentils and discard any stones. Place the lentils and cloves in a large saucepan and cover with water by 2 inches. Over high heat, bring to a boil. Turn the heat to medium low and simmer, uncovered, until the lentils are almost tender, 15 to 25 minutes. Drain the lentils.

2. Heat the olive oil in a large frying pan and cook the red onions until soft, 7 minutes. Add the garlic and crushed red pepper flakes and cook, uncovered, stirring occasionally, for 1 minute. Add the tomatoes and fish stock or clam juice and cook for 2 to 3 minutes. Add the parsley, oregano, and lentils and cook, stirring occasionally, for 2 minutes. Season with lemon juice, salt, and pepper.

continued on p. 160

herb salad

1½ Tbs. extra-virgin olive oil

1 Tbs. freshly squeezed lemon juice

1 clove garlic, minced

Kosher salt and freshly ground black pepper

½ cup fresh flat-leaf parsley leaves, washed and dried

½ cup small fresh basil leaves, washed and dried

½ cup small fresh mint leaves, washed and dried

2 cups fresh arugula leaves, long stems removed, washed and dried

makes 4 cups

1. In a large bowl, whisk together the olive oil, lemon juice, and garlic. Season to taste with salt and pepper.

2. Combine the herbs and arugula in a large bowl. About 5 minutes before serving, add dressing to the greens and toss together. Season with salt and pepper.

crispy salmon with fennel & radicchio salad

2 bulbs endive

1 medium bulb fennel, green feathery tops reserved, cut into paper-thin slices

1 small head radicchio, leaves torn into 2-inch pieces

6 Tbs. extra-virgin olive oil

2 Tbs. freshly squeezed lemon juice

2 anchovy fillets, soaked in cold water for 10 minutes, patted dry, and minced

1 clove garlic, minced

Kosher salt and freshly ground black pepper

6 pieces of salmon fillet (about 1¼ to 1½ pounds total), skin removed

6 lemon wedges, for garnish

serves 6

MY STUDENTS ALWAYS ASK, "HOW DO I COOK FISH SO IT DOESN'T dry out?" Here is the best technique for making salmon that's juicy on the inside and crispy and golden on the outside. All you need is a nonstick pan with a film of olive oil on the bottom. It's simple—sear the salmon on both sides until golden.

Don't be afraid of the anchovies in the salad dressing. Once you soak the anchovies in water for 10 minutes, they won't be as salty or fishy tasting. If you want, omit the anchovies altogether.

1. Cut about a 1-inch tip off the endive diagonally. Turn the endive a quarter of a turn and cut the endive again diagonally. Continue until you have cut the whole endive. Place in a bowl with the fennel and radicchio.

2. In a small bowl, whisk together 4 Tbs. of the olive oil, the lemon juice, anchovies, and garlic. Season with salt and pepper.

3. Heat the remaining 2 Tbs. oil over high heat in a large, nonstick frying pan. Add the salmon and cook until golden and crispy on one side, 3 minutes. Turn the salmon, season with salt and pepper, and continue to cook until golden and crispy on the second side, 2 to 3 minutes.

4. To serve, toss the vinaigrette with the fennel, radicchio, and endive. Divide onto serving plates. Place a piece of salmon along one side, overlapping the salad. Garnish the salmon with the fennel tops and place a lemon wedge on the side. Serve immediately.

SERVING SUGGESTIONS

- Wine pairing: Dry rosé or a Beaujolais
- To start, smear room-temperature triple-cream cheese on warm toasted crostini.
- For dessert, dip marshmallows in warm melted chocolate.

salmon & spring vegetables baked in paper

Kosher salt and freshly ground black pepper

3 small carrots, peeled and cut into 1-inch pieces on the diagonal

3 Tbs. extra-virgin olive oil

6 salmon fillets (6 ounces each), skin removed

1 lemon, thinly sliced (12 slices total)

1 small bunch asparagus, cut into 1-inch pieces on the diagonal

1 cup sugar snap peas, strings removed

12 sprigs fresh tarragon

¼ cup dry white wine, such as Sauvignon Blanc

serves 6

TALK ABOUT A PRETTY PACKAGE. THIS SALMON IS ALL ABOUT ITS unique presentation, which also conveniently happens to be its cooking method. By wrapping the fish, along with a variety of vegetables and herbs, in a parchment pouch, you get a delicately steamed, perfectly moist result. This dish is also totally flexible: Vary the fish, vegetables, and herbs depending on your taste (or what you have in the refrigerator that day).

1. Bring a saucepan of salted water to a boil. Add the carrots and simmer for 3 minutes. Drain and set aside.

2. Heat the oven to 400°F. Cut 6 pieces of parchment paper (or foil) in the shape of a heart, about 20 inches across at the widest part of the heart. Brush liberally with olive oil. Place one piece of salmon on half of the heart and brush the top of the fillet with more olive oil. Season with salt and pepper and place two slices of lemon on each fillet.

3. Divide the carrots, asparagus, and snap peas evenly among the 6 parchment hearts, scattering them on top of the salmon. Place two tarragon sprigs on each fillet. Sprinkle 1 Tbs. of white wine on top of the fish and season with salt and pepper.

continued on p. 164

- Wine pairing: Chardonnay

- Begin your dinner with endive spears filled with smoked salmon and topped with caviar.

- Serve lemon tarragon rice alongside the salmon.

4. To seal each parcel, fold the heart in half and then fold and crease the edges to enclose the salmon and vegetables. Continue folding the paper down over itself until the parcel is completely enclosed.

5. Place the parchment parcels on a baking sheet, seam side down, and put in the oven; bake until well puffed, about 15 minutes. To serve, place one parchment parcel on each plate and snip the center open with scissors.

IN THE KITCHEN filling parchment packets

The parchment needs to be large enough to fully enclose the fish and vegetables. Start with a parchment square that's about 24 inches and cut it into a heart that's 20 inches at its widest point. It's easiest to know where to place the filling if you fold the heart in half (this makes cutting out the heart shape easier, too). Be sure to fold and crease the parchment as you roll up the sides; this helps seal in the liquid.

Place the salmon, vegetables, herbs, and liquid on half of the heart shape about 1 inch from the fold line.

Starting at the rounded edge of the heart, fold over the paper about 1 inch and crease; continue to fold and crease all sides until the fish and vegetables are fully enclosed.

seafood stew with tomatoes & saffron

1 cup dry white wine, such as Sauvignon Blanc

2 cups bottled clam juice

1 pound small red potatoes, halved

1 cup tomatoes (fresh or canned)

3 cloves garlic, chopped

1 tsp. paprika

1 large pinch saffron threads

1 large pinch crushed red pepper flakes

¼ cup chopped fresh flat-leaf parsley, plus sprigs (for garnish)

1 pound fresh clams, scrubbed

1 pound fresh mussels, scrubbed

1 pound firm white fish fillets, such as cod, haddock, monkfish, or sea bass, cut into 1-inch chunks

½ pound large shrimp (31 to 35 per pound), peeled and deveined

Kosher salt and freshly ground black pepper

serves 6

THIS IS MY QUICK AND EASY VERSION OF THE CLASSIC FRENCH bouillabaisse, a traditional Provençal fish stew. If you're one of those people who thinks seafood is difficult to cook, try this dish, which couldn't be simpler. Most seafood has a very short cooking time and, as long as you purchase the freshest fish you can find, you'll get delicious flavor that doesn't need to be messed with too much. Unlike traditional bouillabaisse, this dish uses seasoned white wine, clam juice, and tomatoes as its base, helping to make it quick and easy—and delicious!

1. In a large soup pot over high heat, combine the first 8 ingredients, plus 1 cup water, and bring to a boil. Reduce the heat to medium, cover, and simmer for 20 minutes. Uncover and simmer for another 10 minutes.

2. Add the chopped parsley and clams and cook just until the clams begin to open, 2 to 3 minutes. Add the mussels and cook just until they begin to open, 2 to 3 minutes. (Discard any clams and mussels that do not open.) Place the fish and shrimp on top of the clams and mussels and simmer slowly, covered, until the fish is cooked, 5 minutes. Season with salt and pepper.

3. Ladle soup into bowls and garnish with parsley sprigs and serve.

SERVING SUGGESTIONS

- Wine pairing: Use a good Sauvignon Blanc for the stew, and pour the rest at the table.

- You'll want a loaf of good crusty bread or bruschetta to mop up the broth.

seared scallops with lemon, caper & parsley pesto

FOR THE PESTO

1 Tbs. freshly grated lemon zest

¾ cup chopped fresh
flat-leaf parsley

1 clove garlic, minced

¼ cup capers, rinsed

1½ Tbs. freshly squeezed
lemon juice

Kosher salt and freshly ground
black pepper

3 Tbs. extra-virgin olive oil

FOR THE SCALLOPS

1½ pounds large fresh sea scallops

1 Tbs. extra-virgin olive oil

Kosher salt and freshly ground
black pepper

FOR SERVING

1 bunch of watercress,
stems removed

Lemon wedges, for garnish

serves 6

FOR THOSE OF YOU WHO PURCHASE A WHOLE BUNCH OF PARSLEY
only to use a teaspoon or two in a recipe, this pesto is a great way
to use it up. Not a typical pesto, this version adds the tang of lemon
and capers, making it the perfect complement to seared scallops. It
also works wonders with chicken, pork chops, and flank steak—you
name it. Freeze any leftover pesto in ice cube trays (pop out once
frozen and put in a zip-top bag), so you can have pesto at the ready
whenever you want to make this dish.

Make the pesto

Place the lemon zest, parsley, garlic, capers, and lemon juice in the bowl
of a food processor. Season to taste with salt and pepper. Pulse a few
times to make a rough paste, scraping down the sides of the bowl.
Gradually add the olive oil while continuing to pulse until the mixture is
a thick yet loose paste.

Make the scallops

Remove the muscle from the side of each scallop and discard. In a large,
nonstick frying pan over medium-high heat, warm the oil until almost
rippling. Add the scallops in a single layer. Do not overcrowd the pan—cook
in two batches if necessary. Cook the scallops until golden on one side,
2 minutes. Turn the scallops, season with salt and pepper, and continue
to cook until the scallops are golden and slightly firm to the touch, 2 to
3 minutes. The cooking time depends upon the size of the scallops.

To serve

Divide the scallops among six serving plates. Spoon a dollop of the
pesto over the scallops on each plate, distributing evenly. Top with the
watercress, garnish with lemon wedges, and serve immediately.

- Wine pairing: Viognier

- To start, warm your favorite store-bought flat bread or focaccia, then smear it with fig jam and top with crumbled blue cheese.

- As a side dish, surround the scallops with tiny roasted or grilled red potatoes.

IN THE KITCHEN searing scallops

Once the oil is rippling, add the scallops to the pan (don't crowd them!) and cook until golden on one side, about 2 minutes. Turn them over and continue to cook on the second side until the scallops are golden and slightly firm to the touch, 1 to 2 minutes, depending upon the size of the scallops. Always use fresh scallops, never frozen.

shellfish paella

6 cups chicken stock

1 tsp. saffron threads

2 Tbs. extra-virgin olive oil

½ pound firm dry chorizo, cut into ½-inch slices

1 medium yellow onion, chopped

4 cloves garlic, minced

1 tsp. pimentón or smoked paprika

2 cups short-grain paella rice

5 Tbs. chopped fresh flat-leaf parsley, plus 2 Tbs. for garnish

3 canned whole pimentos or roasted peppers, diced

½ cup dry white wine, such as Sauvignon Blanc

1 Tbs. freshly squeezed lemon juice

1½ tsp. kosher salt

¾ pound large shrimp (31 to 35 per pound), shelled and deveined

1 pound Manila clams, scrubbed

1 pound mussels, scrubbed

½ pound shelled English peas (fresh or frozen)

Lemon slices, for garnish (optional)

serves 6 to 8

PAELLA IS A FLAVORFUL RICE DISH THAT ORIGINATED IN VALENCIA, Spain, along the Mediterranean Sea. I first learned to cook paella in Spain over a large open flame using a paellera, a round, shallow steel pan with handles on either side. I enjoyed the experience so much that I brought a paellera and huge burner home with me. I now love teaching my students the traditional way to make paella on my tiny San Francisco balcony.

While there are many different versions of this dish, the one essential ingredient common to all paella is saffron, which gives it its signature bright orange-yellow hue. This version features a variety of seafood nestled into seasoned rice and baked. One bite and you'll find yourself planning a trip to Spain.

1. Place the stock and saffron in a large saucepan over high heat. Bring to a boil and turn the heat off; set aside.

2. Warm the olive oil in a heavy, 4½-quart, double-handled frying pan, about 12 to 13 inches in diameter. Add the chorizo, onions, garlic, and pimentón to the pan and cook, stirring occasionally, until the onions are soft, 15 minutes. Remove from the pan and set aside. Pour off all but 2 Tbs. of the oil from the pan. Add the rice to the pan and stir to coat it well with the oil. Add the 5 Tbs. of chopped parsley and the diced pimentos or roasted peppers.

3. Heat the oven to 325°F. Bring the chicken stock to a boil, then add it to the frying pan along with the wine, lemon juice, and salt. Stir well and simmer for 5 minutes. Bury the shrimp, clams, and mussels in the rice. Bake, uncovered, until the clams and mussels are open, 15 minutes. (Discard any clams or mussels that don't open.) Place the peas on the top and cook for another 5 minutes. Remove from the oven, cover, and let stand for 5 minutes. Sprinkle with the 2 Tbs. of chopped parsley, garnish with lemon slices if desired, and serve.

- Wine pairing: Fino sherry
- Serve a chunk of Manchego with membrillo, or quince paste, to start.
- For dessert, drizzle Pedro Jiminez sherry over vanilla ice cream.

IN THE KITCHEN deveining shrimp

It's always best to buy shrimp that has not been previously cooked. It's freshest this way, plus it's cheaper. Although deveining is a bit messy, it's easy to do. Be sure you work with a small knife.

Once the shell has been removed, hold the shrimp in one hand with the back of the shrimp facing out. Use the tip of a paring knife to cut down the back to expose the vein.

Gently pull on the black vein to remove it. You might need to use the tip of the knife to nudge it out completely. Discard the vein.

sizzling shrimp with pimentón & sherry

3 Tbs. extra-virgin olive oil

6 cloves garlic, thinly sliced

Large pinch crushed red pepper flakes

2 pounds jumbo shrimp (11 to 15 per pound), peeled and deveined

½ tsp. pimentón or smoked paprika

¾ cup Amontillado or Oloroso sherry

Kosher salt and freshly ground black pepper

½ Tbs. chopped fresh flat-leaf parsley, for garnish

serves 6

SERVING SUGGESTIONS

• Wine pairing: Amontillado sherry

• For a first course, serve some hot, crispy golden potato chunks topped with a garlicky mayonnaise.

• Serve the sizzling shrimp on a bed of rice.

SMOKED PAPRIKA, ALSO CALLED PIMENTÓN, IS A SPICE FREQUENTLY used in Spanish cooking. It is made from ground, dried, red chile peppers and adds a warm, smoky flavor to sautéed shrimp in this bold dish, inspired by one of my trips to the Basque region of Spain. You'll want to use a sweeter sherry for this recipe as the reduced sherry serves to temper the pimentón and add a layer of nutty sweetness that's truly incredible. This dinner is an excellent choice when you're short on time (since the cooking time is just 5 minutes flat) but want something incredibly flavorful.

Heat the oil in a large frying pan over medium-high heat. Add the garlic and red pepper flakes and cook for 15 seconds. Add the shrimp and pimentón, and cook until the shrimp curls and turns pink, 3 minutes. Add the sherry and continue to cook until the sherry reduces by half, 1 minute. Season to taste with salt and pepper. Place in a serving dish, garnish with parsley, and serve immediately.

spicy spaghetti with sautéed fennel & mussels

3 Tbs. extra-virgin olive oil

1 small onion, diced

1 clove garlic, minced

½ tsp. fennel seeds, coarsely ground

2 bulbs fennel

½ cup dry white wine, such as Sauvignon Blanc or Pinot Grigio

½ cup bottled clam juice

Pinch of crushed red pepper flakes

2 pounds mussels, washed well and beards removed

1 pound 100% semolina spaghetti

serves 6

SERVING SUGGESTIONS

• Wine pairing: Falanghina or Arneis

• To start, serve an heirloom tomato salad with caper vinaigrette.

• To finish, drizzle strawberries with reduced balsamic vinegar.

I'VE HAD A FEW STUDENTS COME THROUGH MY COOKING CLASSES claiming they "hate" the taste of fennel. Every single one says something different once they've tasted this dish. Sautéing the fennel bulb until it begins to soften and caramelize brings out its inherent sweetness and mellows its licorice flavor. The mussels then steam in the aromatic stock, releasing a briny sweetness. Tossed with cooked semolina spaghetti, the fennel becomes a beautiful note in a symphony of flavors.

1. Warm the oil in a large frying pan over medium-high heat. Add the onions and cook until soft, 10 minutes. Add the garlic and fennel seeds and cook for 1 minute.

2. Cut the top and bottom off the fennel and reserve the green tops. Chop 2 Tbs. of the tops and reserve. Cut the fennel bulbs into ½-inch pieces, add to the pan, and cook until the fennel begins to soften, 5 minutes. Increase the heat to high, add the white wine, clam juice, and red pepper flakes and simmer until the stock has reduced by half. Add the mussels and cook until they open. Discard any mussels that do not open.

3. In the meantime bring a large pot of salted water to a boil Add the spaghetti and cook until al dente, 8 to 10 minutes, or according to the package directions. Drain the pasta and toss together with the fennel mixture. Place in a large, warm serving bowl and serve immediately.

IN THE PANTRY bottled clam juice

I love cooking shellfish, and I always keep 1 or 2 bottles of clam juice on hand. This clam juice is the perfect substitute for homemade fish stock or fish fumet, both of which can be labor intensive to make. Thanks to its sweet shellfish flavor, bottled clam juice can be your go-to stock when fish or shellfish are involved.

ahi tuna tacos
with avocado crema

FOR THE AVOCADO CREMA

3 ripe avocados

½ cup crème fraîche or sour cream

1 Tbs. freshly squeezed lime juice

¼ tsp. cayenne pepper

Kosher salt and freshly ground
black pepper

FOR THE TUNA

1½ pounds fresh ahi tuna steak,
1¼ inches thick

2 Tbs. mild-flavored oil, such as
vegetable or corn oil

Kosher salt and freshly ground
black pepper

FOR THE TACOS

12 fresh corn tortillas, about
6 inches in diameter

⅛ head red cabbage, very
thinly sliced

⅛ head green cabbage, very
thinly sliced

Sprigs of fresh cilantro, for garnish

Lime wedges, for garnish

makes 12 tacos; serves 6

I LOVE A GOOD FISH TACO. I'LL BE THE FIRST TO ADMIT I'M A
sucker for the fried variety, but that's not something I can (or should)
eat on a regular basis. This version, made with ahi tuna grilled
medium rare and silky, smooth cayenne-spiked avocado crema, is
lighter yet just as satisfying. Wrapped in warm corn tortillas with
crisp, colorful cabbage, this fish taco is simply scrumptious.

Prepare an outdoor grill.

Make the avocado crema
Cut the avocado from top to bottom, going right around the pit. Twist the
two pieces to separate the halves. Tap the blade of your knife into the pit to
lodge the blade in the pit. Twist the blade and remove the pit. Remove the
pit from the knife, being mindful of the blade since the pit can be slippery.
With a large spoon, scoop the pulp flesh away from the skin. Discard the pit
and skin. Place the avocado in the bowl of a food processor and pulse with
the crème fraîche or sour cream. Add the lime juice and cayenne; season
with salt and pepper. Set aside.

Make the tuna
Brush the tuna with the oil and season well with salt and pepper. Cook the
tuna fillets 4 inches from the heat source until light golden on one side, 2 to
3 minutes. Turn and continue to cook on the second side until the outside
is golden but the center is still pink, 2 to 3 minutes (use the tip of a knife
to make a small slit in the tuna to check doneness). Remove from the heat
and break or cut the tuna into ½-inch pieces.

- Drink pairing: Cerveza, margaritas, or ice-cold beer
- Start with warm tortilla chips with tomatillo and avocado salsa.
- Serve grilled pineapple sweetened with brown sugar and doused with añejo tequila (light it and serve while flamed)

To serve

1. Just before serving, warm a nonstick frying pan over medium-high heat. Place the tortillas, one at a time, in the frying pan, turning them over to warm completely on both sides, about 30 seconds total. Place two tortillas on each plate.

2. Spread the avocado crema on the warm tortillas, distributing it evenly. Top with the tuna, distributing it evenly. Toss the red and green cabbage together and place the cabbage on top. Garnish with cilantro and lime wedges. Serve open-face.

grilled yellowtail tuna burgers with wasabi mayonnaise

FOR THE WASABI MAYONNAISE

½ cup mayonnaise

1 clove garlic, minced

1 Tbs. freshly squeezed lemon juice

1½ tsp. wasabi paste

Kosher salt and freshly ground black pepper

FOR THE BURGERS

6 excellent-quality rolls, halved

6 yellowtail tuna fillets (about 4 ounces each, or about 1½ pounds)

2 Tbs. extra-virgin olive oil

Kosher salt and freshly ground black pepper

Pea shoots, for garnish (optional)

Sliced tomatoes, for garnish (optional)

Sliced red onions, for garnish (optional)

Thai Cabbage and Grapefruit Slaw (recipe on p. 178)

serves 6

FRESH TUNA IS BEST WHEN IT IS SEARED JUST UNTIL GOLDEN AND crisp on the outside but remains tender and rare on the inside. Sushi-grade tuna is your best bet when serving tuna rare to medium rare and can be special-ordered at your local fish counter.

For these Asian-inspired burgers, a slathering of spicy wasabi mayonnaise is the perfect complement to the tuna. Serve on your favorite bakery roll.

Make the wasabi mayonnaise

Combine the mayonnaise, garlic, lemon juice, and wasabi paste in a bowl. Mix well and season with salt and pepper.

Make the burgers

1. Heat an outdoor grill. Set the grate 4 inches from the heat source.

2. Grill the rolls and set aside.

3. Brush the tuna with the oil and season with salt and pepper. Grill the tuna until golden on one side, 2 to 3 minutes. Turn the tuna and grill on the second side until golden on the outside and rare to medium rare on the inside, 2 to 3 additional minutes.

4. Place the tuna on the bottom of each roll, topping the tuna with a big dollop of wasabi mayonnaise. Serve immediately, accompanied by pea shoots, tomato slices, and onion slices (if desired) and slaw.

SERVING SUGGESTIONS

• Wine pairing: Albariño

• For dessert, chocolate brownies and mint chocolate chip ice cream.

continued on p. 178

thai cabbage & grapefruit slaw

¼ cup mayonnaise

2 Tbs. extra-virgin olive oil

¼ cup white-wine vinegar

1 Tbs. soy sauce

2 Tbs. fish sauce

½ serrano chile, seeded and minced

2 Tbs. finely grated fresh ginger

2 Tbs. granulated sugar

2 tsp. freshly grated grapefruit zest

Kosher salt and freshly ground black pepper

1 grapefruit

½ head Savoy cabbage (about ¾ pound), cored, quartered, and thinly sliced

½ head red cabbage (about ¾ pound), cored, quartered, and thinly sliced

1 small head radicchio (about ½ pound), cored, quartered, and thinly sliced

6 green onions, white and green parts, thinly sliced on the diagonal

¼ cup chopped fresh cilantro leaves and stems

serves 6

1. Place the mayonnaise, oil, vinegar, soy sauce, fish sauce, serrano chile, ginger, sugar, and grapefruit zest in a small bowl and whisk together. Season with salt and pepper.

2. Using a sharp knife, cut the tops and bottoms off the grapefruit to reveal the colored flesh. Place one of the cut sides down on a work surface. Using a small, sharp knife, cut off the peel and white pith from top to bottom. Turn the fruit to the opposite cut side and remove any white pith. Cut the grapefruit into sections, cutting between the membrane. Discard any seeds.

3. Place the grapefruit sections, cabbages, radicchio, green onions, and cilantro in a bowl. Add the dressing and toss together. Season with salt and pepper.

tilapia with orange & chipotle glaze

½ cup orange marmalade

2 Tbs. freshly squeezed orange juice

1 Tbs. chipotle in adobo, mashed to a paste

Kosher salt

2 Tbs. olive oil

2 pounds fresh tilapia fillets, cut into six 5- to 6-ounce pieces

serves 6

THIS SEAFOOD DISH IS A WONDERFUL EXAMPLE OF HOW A FEW SIMPLE ingredients can come together in just minutes to produce an elegant, delicious meal. Mild-flavored, flaky tilapia is simply seared then slathered in a homemade chipotle-spiked orange marmalade. After a brief stint in a hot oven, the fish is moist and tender and the sweet-spicy glaze perfectly caramelized. Don't tell me that doesn't that make your mouth water!

1. Heat the oven to 375°F and position a rack in the top third of the oven.

2. In a bowl, combine the orange marmalade, orange juice, and chipotle mash. Season with salt.

3. Warm the oil in a large, heavy, ovenproof frying pan over medium-high heat. Make sure the pan is large enough to accommodate 6 tilapia fillets without overlapping; if it's not, you'll need to cook the fish in batches. Add the fish and sear on one side. Turn the fish over and spoon all of the marmalade-chipotle mixture over the top. (If you have to cook the fish in batches, reserve some of the mixture for the second batch.)

4. Place the pan in the top third of the oven and cook until the fish can be easily flaked with a fork, about 4 minutes. Remove from the oven and place on serving plates.

SERVING SUGGESTIONS

- Wine pairing: Viognier or Torrontés
- Grill country bread and top with marinated artichokes and shaved Grana Padano as a starter.

- For dessert, skewer fruit and serve with a sweet mascarpone and Kalúa® dipping sauce.

6

THE
meat OF THE MATTER

THE RECIPES

TECHNIQUES MADE SIMPLE

bruschetta burger with caramelized onions & blue cheese

4½ Tbs. extra-virgin olive oil

3 medium yellow onions, thinly sliced

Kosher salt and freshly ground black pepper

4 ounces blue cheese, crumbled

2 pounds lean ground beef, preferably grass fed

½ cup ricotta cheese

6 slices rustic coarse-textured bread

1 clove garlic, peeled

3 cups arugula

serves 6

THIS DECADENT BURGER CAME ABOUT AS A RECONSTRUCTION OF ONE of my favorite indulgent meals: rib-eye steak with Gorgonzola butter and caramelized onions. I was looking for a way to showcase all of the same delicious flavors without shelling out the big bucks. Instead of rib-eye, I opted for grass-fed ground beef. A touch of ricotta (trust me!) transforms the beef into the most luscious, juicy burger you've ever tasted. Topped with caramelized onions tossed with crumbled blue cheese and served on rustic bread with a hint of peppery arugula, this is one stand-out burger. Cheap and scrumptious. A win-win all around.

1. In a large frying pan, warm 2 Tbs. of the oil over medium heat. Add the yellow onions, cover, and cook for 15 minutes. Remove the cover, season with salt and pepper, and continue to cook until the onions are very soft and just begin to turn golden, 20 to 30 minutes. Let the onions cool, then crumble the blue cheese into the mixture and stir together gently. Set aside.

2. Place the beef and ricotta in a bowl and mix together. Season with 1 tsp. salt and ½ tsp. pepper. Form 6 patties that are about 3 inches across.

3. Heat an outdoor charcoal grill. Set the grate 4 inches from the heat source.

4. Grill the bread until light golden on both sides. Rub the toasted bread on one side well with the peeled garlic. Brush the bread with 2 Tbs. of the oil and set aside. Grill the burgers for 4 to 5 minutes per side until medium rare. To check for doneness, there should be slight resistance when the center of the burger is pressed gently. Place one slice of grilled bread on each serving plate and top with a burger.

- Wine pairing: Zinfandel
- As a perfect side dish, make some crispy, oven French fries. If you want to keep it even simpler, serve some of your favorite potato chips.

5. Toss the arugula with the remaining ½ Tbs. olive oil and a pinch of salt. Spoon the caramelized onions and blue cheese on top of each burger, dividing evenly; garnish with arugula, and serve immediately.

AT THE MARKET grass-fed beef

Grass-fed beef is exactly that—beef that has been raised in the pasture on grass as opposed to corn or other grains. Grass-fed beef is lower in saturated fats and slightly higher in Omega-3 fatty acids than other kinds of beef. It's a leaner choice, fairly priced, absolutely delicious, and worth every penny.

vietnamese cold noodle bowl with grilled pork & basil

2 Tbs. soy sauce

1 Tbs. light brown sugar

5 Tbs. fish sauce or nam pla

2 Tbs. vegetable oil

Kosher salt and freshly ground black pepper

1 pork tenderloin (about 1½ pounds) cut into ½-inch thick slices

3 Tbs. sugar

5 Tbs. freshly squeezed lime juice

½ jalapeño, seeded and minced

1 clove garlic, minced

One 8- to 9-ounce package dried rice vermicelli noodles

2 cups bean sprouts

1 medium English cucumber, halved lengthwise, seeded, and thinly sliced

1 cup finely shredded carrots

1 cup fresh basil leaves, preferably Thai

½ cup fresh cilantro leaves

½ cup fresh mint leaves

1 small head romaine, leaves separated and cut crosswise into ½-inch slices

½ cup dry-roasted peanuts, coarsely chopped

serves 6

THIS DISH IS A BIT OF A DEPARTURE FROM THE TYPE OF CUISINE I traditionally prepare at home, but I was tired of paying upwards of $15 at my local Vietnamese restaurant to enjoy this delicious noodle bowl, so I decided to re-create it at home. Boy, was I excited by the results. The Asian-inspired marinade infuses the pork tenderloin with flavor and ensures the lean meat stays tender on the grill. The dressing is made with fish sauce, lime juice, jalapeño, and garlic. Served atop a bed of translucent rice noodles, crisp vegetables, and herbs, this meal is absolutely exquisite.

1. In a medium shallow bowl, combine the soy sauce, light brown sugar, 1 Tbs. of the fish sauce, 1 Tbs. of oil, and black pepper to taste in a bowl. Add the pork and stir together to make sure the pork is completely covered. Cover and refrigerate for 1 to 2 hours.

2. While the pork is marinating, make the dressing. Stir together the remaining 4 Tbs. fish sauce, the sugar, lime juice, jalapeño, garlic, and ¼ cup water. Set aside.

3. Cook the noodles in a large pot of boiling salted water until just tender and turning white, separating often with a fork, about 4 minutes. Drain and run under cold water to cool. Arrange the noodles in the center of a large serving bowl. Top with the bean sprouts, cucumbers, carrots, basil, cilantro, mint, and lettuce.

4. Heat an outdoor grill and set the grate 4 inches from the heat source.

5. Brush the grill with the remaining 1 Tbs. of oil. Grill the pork until golden and cooked through, 3 to 4 minutes per side. Let cool for 3 to 4 minutes. Place the pork on the top of the noodles and vegetables. Stir the dressing then drizzle over the pork and vegetables; sprinkle the peanuts on top and serve.

- Wine pairing: Riesling or Torrontés
- Serve with a salad of snow peas, pea shoots, and English peas dressed with rice vinegar, tamari, and corn oil.

IN THE PANTRY fish sauce

Fish sauce is an essential ingredient in the Thai pantry. Made from fermented anchovies, salt, and water, fish sauce, or nam pla, adds incredible richness and depth to any dish. It is the staple ingredient responsible for the mouth-watering flavor in many Asian dishes.

grilled steak & potato salad

2 pounds small red potatoes

9 Tbs. extra-virgin olive oil

Kosher salt and freshly ground black pepper

½ cup chopped fresh flat-leaf parsley

3 Tbs. chopped fresh chives

2 tsp. chopped fresh oregano

2 cloves garlic, minced

2 rib-eye steaks (about 2 pounds total), fat trimmed

2 cups tender baby salad greens

serves 6

SERVING SUGGESTIONS

- Wine pairing: Cabernet Sauvignon
- To start, serve a fresh-vegetable minestrone drizzled with fruity virgin olive oil.
- For dessert, toss fresh summer raspberries with softly whipped cream and drizzle the top with cassis.

WE'VE ALL EATEN STEAK AND POTATOES, BUT THE CLASSIC COMBINATION generally means steak with some sort of potato side dish. Let's be honest, though—the best bites always include a bit of both elements. In this version, I'm not messing around. Grilled rib-eyes and grilled red potatoes come together in a single dish, tossed with green onions, salad greens, and a variety of fresh herbs. The result is pretty spectacular, if I do say so myself.

1. Heat the oven to 375°F. Wash the potatoes and place in a 9 x 13-inch baking dish. Drizzle with 1 Tbs. of the oil, season with salt and pepper, cover with foil, and bake until the potatoes can be easily skewered with a knife or fork, 50 to 60 minutes.

2. In a bowl, stir together the parsley, chives, oregano, garlic, and 5 Tbs. of the oil. Season with salt and pepper.

3. Heat an outdoor grill and set the grate 4 inches from the heat source.

4. Brush the steaks with 1 Tbs. olive oil. Season with salt and pepper. Place the steaks on the grill and cook on one side until browned, 4 to 5 minutes. Turn the steaks and continue to cook until medium rare, 4 to 5 minutes. You can test this for doneness using an instant-read thermometer. It should register 130° to 135°F for medium rare. Remove from the grill, cover loosely with foil, and let rest while you grill the potatoes.

5. Cut the potatoes in half. Place the remaining 2 Tbs. of oil in a small bowl. Dip the cut side of the potatoes into the oil and place on the grill. Grill until the potatoes are hot and have golden brown grill marks, 5 to 7 minutes. Remove from the grill and place in a large serving bowl. Cut the steaks on the diagonal into thin slices. Add the salad greens, herb mixture, and beef to the potatoes and toss together. Season with salt and pepper. Serve immediately.

harissa-rubbed pork tenderloin with mint & cumin yogurt

½ cup prepared harissa

Kosher salt and freshly ground black pepper

1 Tbs. olive oil

2 pork tenderloins (about 1¼ pounds each), trimmed and excess fat removed

1 cup plain Greek yogurt

¼ cup chopped fresh mint leaves

1 tsp. ground cumin

½ tsp. fresh squeezed lemon juice

serves 6

SERVING SUGGESTIONS

- Wine pairing: Beaujolais
- As a side dish, serve couscous.
- For dessert, serve fresh melon drizzled with honey and topped with toasted pistachios.

HARISSA IS A NORTH AFRICAN HOT CHILE SAUCE THAT SERVES AS A smoky hot rub for pork tenderloin in this seriously simple dinner. It can be found prepared at specialty stores and most grocery stores around the county. It's amazing how one little jar can turn out such a delicious dinner with virtually no effort! Served with yogurt flavored with earthy cumin and bright mint to temper the heat, this is a meal you will fall in love with. Try this recipe with chicken breasts instead of pork, too.

1. Heat the oven to 425°F.

2. In a large bowl, stir together the harissa, 1 tsp. salt, and ½ tsp. pepper. Set aside.

3. Warm the oil in a large, ovenproof frying pan over medium-high heat. Add the pork and brown, turning occasionally, until golden on all sides, 6 to 8 minutes total. Remove the pork from the pan.

4. When the pork is cool enough to handle, place it in the bowl with the harissa mixture and turn to coat. Transfer the pork back into the ovenproof frying pan, place in the oven, and cook to an internal temperature of 155°F, 15 to 20 minutes. Let rest for 5 to 10 minutes before slicing.

5. For the dipping sauce, mix together the yogurt, mint, cumin, and lemon juice in a small bowl. Season with salt and pepper.

6. Slice each tenderloin into 1-inch-thick pieces and serve with sauce on the side.

braised lamb shanks with spring vegetables & mint gremolata

2 Tbs. extra-virgin olive oil

6 lamb shanks (½ to ¾ pound each)

Kosher salt and freshly ground black pepper

Unbleached all-purpose flour, for dusting

1 pound peeled carrots

1 medium yellow onion, cut into ¼-inch dice

1 stalk celery, cut into ¼-inch dice

1 Tbs. tomato paste

4 cloves garlic, minced

1½ cups dry white wine, such as Sauvignon Blanc

2 cups low-sodium chicken stock

1 Tbs. lemon zest

2 Tbs. freshly chopped mint

½ pound sugar snap peas, ends and strings removed

serves 6

AS WITH MOST BRAISES, THIS DISH BEGINS WITH A BIT OF UP-FRONT work, browning the lamb shanks and preparing a flavorful braising liquid. The lamb then does its own thing for a few hours, simmering until the meat is falling off the bone. So what sets this dish apart from any other braise? Beautiful spring vegetables, cooked in the puréed braising liquid, add vibrancy to the meal, while the bright, fresh flavors of mint, lemon zest, and garlic in the gremolata, a simple Italian herb condiment, provide a lovely counterbalance to the decadent braised meat.

1. In a deep, heavy stew pot, heat the oil over medium-high heat. Season the lamb shanks well with salt and pepper and dust with flour, tapping off the excess.

2. Brown the lamb shanks on all sides, 10 to 15 minutes total. Remove from the pan and set aside. Cut two of the carrots into ¼-inch dice. Add the diced carrots, onions, and celery to the pot and cook, uncovered, until the onions are soft, 10 minutes. Add the tomato paste and three-quarters of the garlic and stir for 1 minute. Stir in the wine and chicken stock and return the lamb shanks to the pot. Increase the heat to high and bring to a boil. Reduce the heat to low and simmer, covered, until the lamb begins to fall from the bone and the shanks can be easily skewered, 2 to 2½ hours. Season with salt and pepper.

3. In the meantime, make the gremolata by combining the lemon zest, mint, and remaining garlic. Set aside.

4. When the lamb is tender and almost falls off the bone, remove the shanks with tongs and place on a platter. Cover with foil to keep warm.

continued on p. 190

- Wine pairing: Barolo or Cabernet Sauvignon
- To round out this main course, serve with Israeli couscous scented with lemon.

5. Cut the remaining carrots into 1½-inch lengths.

6. Skim the fat from the braising liquid and discard. Place the sauce in a blender and purée on high speed until very smooth, 1 to 2 minutes. Return the sauce to the pot and bring to a simmer over medium heat. Reduce the heat to low, add the carrots, and cook, uncovered, until tender, 10 minutes. Add the sugar snap peas and cook until bright green, 3 to 4 minutes. Return the lamb to the pot and simmer, uncovered, until it is hot and the sauce is bubbling, 8 to 10 minutes.

7. To serve, place a lamb shank on each plate and top with a spoonful of sauce. Sprinkle the gremolata onto the top and serve immediately.

IN THE KITCHEN braising

When braising, it is very important to brown the meat well at the start. This gives the meat a golden crust that "melts" when liquid is added and gives flavor to the finished sauce. Be sure, though, that you do not burn the bottom of the pan; the bits on the bottom should range from golden brown to brown. Once you've browned your meat, remove it from the pan and set aside on a platter, uncovered.

Add any aromatics called for and cook until soft. This also contributes to the flavor of the finished sauce. (Some recipes might also call for optional flavoring ingredients, like tomato paste, thyme sprigs, bay leaves, and dry mushrooms.) Add wine to the pan and scrape up the brown bits on the bottom of the pan. This is called deglazing. Add the meat back to the pan along with liquid, either stock or water, to almost cover. Cover and simmer until the meat is fork-tender, which means that you can almost cut the meat with a fork—it's that tender.

honey-glazed pork chops with orange & cardamom

16 cardamom pods

6 pork rib or loin bone-in chops, at least 1 inch thick (about 8 to 10 ounces each)

3 oranges

Kosher salt and freshly ground black pepper

1 tsp. olive oil

3 Tbs. honey

serves 6

DID ANYONE ELSE GROW UP EATING PORK CHOPS THAT WERE SO dry you had to wash them down with a glass of milk? These are *not* those chops. By brining the pork in an aromatic orange and cardamom marinade, you ensure a perfectly tender and juicy piece of meat. These pork chops are then pan-seared and brushed with honey, which caramelizes perfectly when finished in the oven. Not only does this dish boast incredible sweet-savory flavor, but it's also simple to prepare, with just five ingredients total. Doesn't get much better than that.

1. For the wet marinade, place the cardamom pods in a spice grinder and grind to make a rough dust. Place the cardamom, pork chops, the zest from 1 orange, juice from all of the oranges, 1 Tbs. salt, and a large pinch of black pepper in a large zip-top bag. Close the bag and shake gently to distribute the spices and orange zest evenly around the pork chops. Place the bag in the refrigerator for 1 hour, shaking the bag gently halfway through the marinating.

2. After 1 hour, drain the pork chops and discard the wet marinade. Pat the pork chops with paper towels until they are completely dry.

3. Warm the oil in a large, ovenproof, nonstick frying pan over medium-high heat until almost rippling. Add the pork and cook until golden, 1 minute per side. Reduce the heat to medium low, cover, and cook the pork chops for 5 minutes. Turn the pork chops over and continue to cook, covered, for an additional 4 to 6 minutes, depending upon the thickness of the pork chops. The pork is done when the meat is firm and has resistance but is not hard when you press with your finger. You can also test the meat with an instant-read meat thermometer to see that the internal temperature is 145° to 155°F when inserted into the center of the meat.

- Wine pairing: Riesling or Gewürztraminer
- A wonderful accompaniment would be roasted root vegetables like butternut squash, carrots, turnip, parsnips, and rutabaga.
- For dessert, top frozen vanilla yogurt with sautéed pineapple, raisins, brown sugar, and dark rum.

4. Heat the broiler.

5. Brush the pork with the honey and place the pan under the broiler so that the tops of the pork chops are 4 inches from the heat source. Broil until sizzling and golden, 30 seconds.

6. Remove the pork from the pan and let rest for 5 minutes before serving.

IN THE PANTRY how long do spices keep?

Spices, like eggs and milk, have a shelf life. For spices, it's about 6 months. After that, they lose their potency, aroma, and flavor. It's best to buy small amounts of spices and replenish them regularly. If you want to prolong the life of your spices, buy whole seeds and pods like cardamom (as in this recipe) as well as cumin, fennel, and coriander. Using them takes a little more work since you have to grind them, but the flavor will last much longer, even up to a year. And if you want even more flavor, you can toast them in a dry pan and then grind them.

rigatoni with ricotta meatballs in smoky tomato sauce

FOR THE SAUCE

2 Tbs. extra-virgin olive oil

1 red onion, left whole, peeled

5 cups canned fire-roasted tomatoes, peeled, seeded, and diced

3 Tbs. tomato paste

1 tsp. sugar

4 sprigs fresh basil

Kosher salt and freshly ground black pepper

FOR THE MEATBALLS

1 Tbs. extra-virgin olive oil, plus more for the baking sheet

½ small yellow onion, minced

1 clove garlic, minced

½ cup fresh breadcrumbs

3 Tbs. milk

¾ tsp. dried oregano

1 Tbs. tomato paste

½ pound ground pork

½ pound grass-fed ground beef

¾ cup ricotta

1 egg, whisked

1½ cups freshly grated Parmigiano-Reggiano

Kosher salt and freshly ground black pepper

1 pound dry rigatoni

serves 6

A RIFF ON THE CLASSIC DINNERTIME FAVORITE SPAGHETTI AND meatballs, this dish features smoky tomato sauce made with "fire-roasted" tomatoes. Pork and beef meatballs are baked and then simmered in the sauce, infusing the tender meatballs with subtle heat. And if you're wondering why I add ricotta to the meatballs, you just have to try them for yourself. They simply melt in your mouth with lusciousness.

Rigatoni replaces traditional spaghetti, and the hollow tubes of pasta fill with sauce, bursting with flavor as you dig into this delicious dish. If you're a spaghetti and meatball lover like me, this one is for you!

Make the sauce

Heat the oil in a large pot over medium-high heat. Add the red onion, tomatoes, 1 cup water, tomato paste, and sugar. With the back of a chef's knife, tap the sprigs of basil to release their juices. Add the basil and salt and pepper to taste to the pot and bring to a boil. Reduce the heat to low and simmer, uncovered, until it reduces by one-quarter, about 1 hour. Remove the basil sprigs and onion and discard.

Make the meatballs

1. Heat the oven to 400°F.

2. Heat the remaining 1 Tbs. olive oil in a frying pan over medium heat. Add the yellow onions and cook, stirring occasionally, until soft, 7 minutes. Add the garlic and continue to cook, stirring occasionally, until the garlic perfumes the air, 30 to 60 seconds. Remove from the pan and place the onions and garlic in a bowl.

continued on p. 196

• Wine pairing: Sangiovese

• Start with a Caesar salad.

• For dessert, serve peaches or any fresh seasonal fruit, doused with Moscato, an Italian sparkling wine.

3. In a second bowl, add the breadcrumbs and milk and stir together to moisten the breadcrumbs. Squeeze the breadcrumbs gently to get rid of the excess milk and add them to the onions and garlic. Discard the excess milk. Add the oregano, tomato paste, pork, beef, ricotta, egg, and ½ cup of the Parmigiano-Reggiano and mix together until well combined. Season with salt and pepper.

4. Form the mixture into 30 meatballs about 1¼ inches in diameter. Place on an oiled baking sheet and bake until brown on the outside, 10 to 15 minutes.

Finish the dish

1. After the tomato sauce has cooked for 1 to 1¼ hours, add the meatballs and continue to cook until the sauce thickens slightly and the meatballs are cooked, 30 minutes. Stir gently and occasionally. If the sauce gets too thick, add additional water.

2. Bring a large pot of salted water to a boil. Add the rigatoni and boil until al dente, 8 to 12 minutes, or according to the package directions. Drain and toss the rigatoni with the tomato sauce and meatballs. Place in a large bowl and garnish with the remaining 1 cup of Parmigiano-Reggiano; serve immediately.

IN THE KITCHEN making meals ahead

When you know you're going to have a busy week, a good strategy to ensure a delicious home-cooked meal is to make something ahead of time that doesn't take long to reheat. I do this often, and this dish is a perfect example. You can make the sauce and meatballs a day in advance, then when you're ready to serve, cook the pasta and gently warm the sauce and meatballs.

grilled skirt steak with tomato & arugula salad

2 Tbs. balsamic vinegar

4 Tbs. extra-virgin olive oil

1 clove garlic, minced

Kosher salt and freshly ground black pepper

2 pounds skirt steak

3 cups multicolored cherry tomatoes, halved

6 cups arugula

serves 6

SKIRT STEAK IS AN EXCELLENT CHOICE FOR A CUT OF BEEF. NOT ONLY is it full of rich flavor, but it's also very economical. Because it has a tendency to be a tougher cut, the trick is to cook it on the rare side of medium rare. The other trick is to serve the steak sliced very thinly against the grain. I love topping grilled meat with a big heaping salad. This simple one of arugula and cherry tomatoes in balsamic vinaigrette makes a stunning presentation.

1. Heat an outdoor grill and position the grill grate 4 to 5 inches from the heat source.

2. In a large bowl, whisk together the vinegar, 3 Tbs. of the oil, and the garlic. Season with salt and pepper.

3. Brush or rub the remaining 1 Tbs. of oil on the steak. Season well with salt and pepper. Grill the steak until it is charred on the outside, about 4 minutes per side. When you press it with your fingertip, there should be a little resistance. You can also check the temperature by inserting an instant-read thermometer into the thickest part; it's done when the thermometer reads 130°F. Transfer the meat to a cutting board, cover loosely with foil, and let rest for 5 minutes. Thinly slice the steak across the grain and transfer to a large platter.

4. Whisk the vinaigrette again and add the tomatoes and arugula. Toss together. Place the salad on top of the beef and serve immediately.

SERVING SUGGESTIONS

- Wine pairing: Sangiovese
- As a first course, serve breadsticks wrapped with prosciutto.
- For dessert, serve cherries and zabaglione (an Italian custard made from egg yolks, wine, and sugar).

lamb sirloin salad with feta & roasted cherry tomatoes

3 Tbs. freshly squeezed lemon juice

4 tsp. chopped fresh oregano

1 clove garlic, minced

½ cup olive oil

Kosher salt and freshly ground black pepper

3 lamb sirloin steaks (about 8 ounces each)

1 head escarole, torn into 2- to 3-inch pieces

2 cups Roasted Cherry Tomatoes (recipe on the facing page)

½ English cucumber, peeled, seeded, and diced

½ red onion, diced

½ cup crumbled feta cheese

½ cup Kalamata olives

2 tsp. chopped fresh mint

serves 6

FOR SOME REASON, PEOPLE TEND TO SHY AWAY FROM COOKING LAMB at home. Just as simple in its preparation as beef, this lamb sirloin is marinated, then grilled and served atop a crisp Mediterranean salad inspired by my travels to Greece. The contrasting flavors of bitter escarole, sweet roasted cherry tomatoes, and salty feta play beautifully with the earthy grilled lamb. Be careful with this salad: It may spur you into calling your travel agent.

1. To make the marinade and vinaigrette, combine the lemon juice, 2 tsp. of the oregano, and the garlic in a small bowl. Whisk in the oil to form an emulsion. Season to taste with salt and pepper.

2. Pour half of the marinade over the lamb and turn to coat. Allow the lamb to marinate for 10 minutes. Reserve the rest of the mixture to use as a vinaigrette.

3. Heat an outdoor grill and set the grate 4 inches from the heat source.

4. Remove the meat from the marinade and lightly pat dry, leaving some of the marinade. Grill the lamb, turning occasionally, until the internal temperature reaches 130°F, about 5 to 7 minutes per side. Remove the meat from the grill and allow to rest for 10 minutes.

5. In the meantime, combine the escarole, tomatoes, cucumbers, and onions in a large serving bowl and toss with the reserved vinaigrette. Slice the lamb against the grain into ½-inch slices and place on top of the vegetables. Sprinkle the feta on top. Garnish with the olives, chopped mint, and the remaining 2 tsp. oregano.

• Wine pairing: Pinot Noir

• For a first course, serve store-bought pita chips and hummus.

• For dessert, serve fresh orange sections with toasted almonds and vanilla Greek yogurt.

AT THE MARKET feta

Feta can be made from goat, sheep, or cow milk or a combination. When buying feta, look for Greek barrel-aged feta. The taste of this full-flavored type far exceeds that from any other country.

roasted cherry tomatoes

3 cups cherry tomatoes

2 Tbs. extra-virgin olive oil

Kosher salt

makes 2 cups

1. Heat the oven to 400°F.

2. Place the tomatoes on a baking sheet and drizzle with the oil. Toss together and season with salt. Spread the tomatoes in a single layer and roast in the oven until the tomatoes are soft, 15 to 20 minutes. Let cool.

grilled skirt steak
with chimichurri

1 packed cup fresh flat-leaf parsley

½ packed cup fresh cilantro leaves

3 cloves garlic, coarsely chopped

2 tsp. chopped fresh oregano

1 shallot, quartered

Pinch of crushed red pepper flakes

6 Tbs. extra-virgin olive oil

1½ Tbs. sherry vinegar

2 tsp. freshly squeezed lemon juice

Kosher salt and freshly ground
black pepper

2 pounds skirt steak

serves 6

CHIMICHURRI, A SLIGHTLY SPICY ARGENTINIAN GREEN HERB SAUCE, does double duty in this recipe as a marinade as well as a sauce for the finished steak. The freshness of the herbs plays perfectly against the flavors of smoky, grilled meat.

1. To make the chimichurri sauce, place the parsley, cilantro, garlic, oregano, shallots, red pepper flakes, oil, vinegar, and lemon juice in a blender or food processor. Pulse until it begins to get smooth but has some texture. Season with salt and pepper.

2. Score the steak by making ¼-inch cuts about an inch apart across the grain of the meat. Place the meat in a large zip-top bag with 3 Tbs. of the chimichurri sauce. Shake the bag and massage the sauce over the steak. Let marinate in the refrigerator for 2 to 3 hours. Place the remaining chimichurri sauce in the refrigerator and save for serving with the meat.

3. When ready for dinner, heat an outdoor grill; position the grill grates 4 to 5 inches from the heat source.

4. Remove the steak from the zip-top bag and sprinkle with salt and pepper. Grill until the meat is charred on the outside, about 4 minutes per side. Transfer the meat to a cutting board and let rest covered loosely with foil for 5 minutes. Thinly slice the steak across the grain and place on a platter. Serve immediately, passing the chimichurri sauce at the table.

SERVING SUGGESTIONS

- Wine pairing: Tempranillo or Malbec.

- Serve with oven-fried potatoes and steamed broccolini.

IN THE KITCHEN how to grill steak

Grilling meat is a simple way to get you out of the hot kitchen in the summer. It's best to start with room-temperature meat (it usually takes 30 minutes to bring steak to room temperature).

Make sure that your grill is set to medium high. To check the temperature, hold your hand 4 to 5 inches from the heat source. It should feel very hot in about 4 seconds. Set the grate 4 inches from the heat source and make sure it's very hot before you put the meat on the grill.

Oil the piece of meat as opposed to oiling the grill. Place the meat on the grill and grill until golden and caramelized on one side, 4 to 5 minutes. Turn the meat and season well. Continue to cook on the second side until medium rare, another 4 to 5 minutes.

How do you really know when steak is done? The best way to tell is to poke it with your fingertips. Place your thumb next to your first finger without any pressure. Feel the muscle at the base of your thumb. It's very soft and spongy. That is what rare feels like, which is meat cooked to 120° to 125°F. Now press your thumb next to your first finger with a little pressure. Feel the muscle? It has some resistance. That's medium rare, about 130° to 135°F. Now press your thumb to your first finger with force and feel the muscle. It's very hard. That's well done, about 150° to 155°F.

my mom's meatloaf
with hot-and-sour ketchup

FOR THE MEATLOAF

¾ cup fresh breadcrumbs

½ cup milk

1 Tbs. olive oil

1 medium yellow onion, minced

1½ pounds grass-fed ground beef

½ pound ground pork

1 cup ricotta or cottage cheese

1 clove garlic, minced

3 Tbs. chopped fresh
flat-leaf parsley

Kosher salt and freshly ground
black pepper

FOR THE HOT-AND-SOUR
KETCHUP

⅓ cup prepared ketchup

3 Tbs. sugar

¼ cup white-wine vinegar

1 Tbs. soy sauce

¼ tsp. cayenne

3½ tsp. cornstarch mixed with
3 Tbs. cold water

serves 6

NOSTALGIC REINCARNATIONS OF CLASSIC COMFORT FOODS ARE popping up everywhere these days. Maybe it's the down economy and a yearning for better times from the past, but it seems you can't go out to dinner without seeing chicken pot pie, macaroni and cheese, or meatloaf on the menu. All of these throwback dishes had me craving my favorite meatloaf—my mom's.

I'm a fourth-generation chef, following in the footsteps of my great-grandmother, grandfather, and mom, so you have to understand that my mom is a rock star in the kitchen, and her meatloaf cannot be beat. With ricotta and milk-soaked breadcrumbs mixed in with beef, pork, herbs, and aromatics, this meatloaf is incredibly moist and flavorful. And then there's the homemade hot-and-sour ketchup. To die for. Let's just say this dinner is an all-around winner. Thanks, Mom.

Make the meatloaf

1. Heat the oven to 400°F.

2. Place the breadcrumbs in a bowl and add the milk. Stir together until well mixed. Set aside.

3. Heat the oil in a frying pan over medium heat. Add the onions and cook until soft, 10 minutes. Place the onions in a medium bowl with the beef, pork, ricotta or cottage cheese, garlic, parsley, 1 tsp. salt, and ½ tsp. pepper. Squeeze the breadcrumbs lightly to remove any excess milk; discard the milk. Add the breadcrumbs to the beef and pork mixture and mix well.

4. Pack the meat mixture into a 5 x 9-inch loaf pan. Bake until a meat thermometer reads 155°F, 45 to 50 minutes.

- Wine pairing: Zinfandel
- Serve a side dish of baked potatoes topped with Greek yogurt, chives, and green onions or brown-sugar-roasted acorn squash.

Make the ketchup

Heat the prepared ketchup, sugar, 1/3 cup of water, the vinegar, soy sauce, and cayenne in a small saucepan over medium-high heat, stirring occasionally. As soon as the mixture comes to a boil, whisk in the cornstarch mixture. Stir constantly until the ketchup mixture thickens, 30 seconds. Remove from the heat and let cool.

To serve

When the meatloaf is done, remove it from the oven and let stand for 15 minutes. Cut into ¾-inch slices and serve immediately with the ketchup sauce in a small bowl on the side.

IN THE KITCHEN   how to make meatloaf moist

Do you want to make your meatloaf, burgers, or meatballs incredibly juicy and moist? Add ½ to ¾ cup of cottage cheese or ricotta per pound of meat to the meatloaf mixture. During the cooking, the cottage cheese or ricotta melts and makes the finished dish juicy.

moroccan merguez
lamb burgers

1¾ pounds grass-fed ground lamb

6 ounces pancetta

6 cloves garlic, minced

1½ Tbs. paprika

1½ tsp. ground cumin

1½ tsp. prepared harissa, more
for garnish

½ tsp. ground cloves

½ tsp. ground cinnamon

¼ tsp. ground nutmeg

Kosher salt and freshly ground
black pepper

¼ cup chopped fresh cilantro

Yogurt, Cucumber & Ginger Sauce
(recipe on the facing page)

6 hamburger buns (optional)

serves 6

ANYONE WHO KNOWS ME KNOWS I HAVE A LOVE AFFAIR WITH LAMB.
I even had a custom spit-roaster installed on the hearth in my
kitchen, which allows me to roast leg of lamb on a regular basis.
This burger is just as delicious as any beef or turkey burger and
gives me my lamb fix in no time flat. It tastes just like the fresh
merguez sausage made in Morocco—one bite and I'm immediately
transported to magical Marrakech, one of my favorite places in
the world.

1. Place about a quarter of the ground lamb, the pancetta, and garlic in
a food processor and process until ground well. Add the paprika, cumin,
1½ tsp. harissa, the cloves, cinnamon, nutmeg, 1½ tsp. salt, and 1 tsp.
pepper and pulse several times until well mixed. Add the remaining lamb
and the cilantro and pulse a few times.

2. To test for flavor, heat a small frying pan over medium heat. Make a
small thin patty with a walnut size piece of the mixture and cook until
done, 3 minutes. Let cool. Taste and season with salt, pepper, and/or
additional spices if needed.

3. Heat an outdoor grill and set the grate 4 inches from the heat source.

4. Form the mixture into 6 patties. Grill the burgers until golden on
one side, 4 to 5 minutes. Turn the burgers and continue to cook until
golden on the second side and medium rare, 3 to 5 minutes. To check the
burgers, press the center gently; there should be a little resistance.

5. To serve, place a lamb burger on each serving plate and top with
Yogurt, Cucumber & Ginger Sauce. Garnish with a small dollop of harrisa
alongside. Serve with buns, if desired.

- **Wine pairing:** Cabernet Sauvignon
- For a first course, serve an arugula and fennel salad dressed with orange zest, orange juice, and olive oil.
- For dessert, grill fresh figs, top with mascarpone and honey, and sprinkle with toasted pine nuts.

AT THE MARKET ground lamb

You can buy ground lamb at your butcher shop or supermarket. If there isn't any available, ask your butcher to grind it for you. I like lamb ground from the leg if possible. And if lamb is not your favorite meat, you can substitute ground turkey, chicken, pork, or beef or a combination.

yogurt, cucumber & ginger sauce

1 cup Greek yogurt

½ English cucumber, peeled, seeded, cut into ¼-inch dice, and drained

1 tsp. lemon zest

1½ Tbs. grated fresh ginger

1 clove garlic, minced

Kosher salt

makes 1½ cups

Place all the ingredients, except the salt, in a small bowl and stir together. Season with salt.

oven-roasted sausages with riesling, apples & pears

2 Tbs. unsalted butter

1 Tbs. brown sugar

3 Bosc pears (about 1½ pounds), peeled, halved, and cored

3 Granny Smith apples (about 1½ pounds), peeled, halved, and cored

Kosher salt

1 cup freshly squeezed orange juice, from about 2 to 3 oranges, or store-bought prepared orange juice

1 cup late-harvest wine, such as Riesling or Gewürztraminer

1 tsp. grated orange zest

2 slices fresh ginger

2 whole cloves

1 cinnamon stick

⅛ tsp. anise seed, crushed

9 sweet Italian pork sausages (about 2 pounds), pricked with a fork

serves 6

SERVING SUGGESTIONS

• Wine pairing: Riesling or Gewürztraminer

• For a first course, serve roasted butternut squash soup garnished with honey-pecan butter.

• Serve rum raisin and butter cookies for dessert.

PREPARING THIS DISH WILL FILL YOUR HOME WITH THE MOST intoxicating aroma ever. The smell alone may be enough to inspire the occasional home cook to prepare dinner on a regular basis. A mixture of orange juice and wine is infused with ginger, cinnamon, cloves, and anise seed, then poured over sautéed apples, pears, and sweet Italian sausage and baked. The meal tastes just as wonderful as it smells.

By the way, don't limit sausages to this recipe—there are many excellent quality types at the market these days, everything from hot and spicy to sweet and aromatic. And the best part is that they can be prepared in minutes, making dinner almost instantaneous. For this recipe, use a sweeter variety sausage for best results.

1. Heat the oven to 375°F.

2. Melt the butter in a large frying pan over medium heat. Add the brown sugar and cook until it is melted. Add the pears and apples, cut side down, in a single layer, and cook until they are golden brown, 5 to 7 minutes. Remove from the heat and place the pears and apples in a large baking dish in a single layer. Season with salt.

3. In the meantime, add the orange juice, late-harvest wine, orange zest, ginger, cloves, cinnamon stick, and anise seed to the frying pan over high heat. Bring to a boil and immediately remove from the heat. Discard the ginger, cinnamon stick, and cloves.

4. Add the sausages to the baking dish with the pears and apples. Pour the orange juice and wine mixture over the pears, apples, and sausages and season with salt. Cover loosely with foil and bake until the sausages are cooked and the pears and apples are tender but still hold their shape, 25 to 35 minutes.

5. To serve, cut each sausage in half on the diagonal. Place 3 pieces of sausage and half of a pear and apple on each plate. Drizzle with the pan juices and serve immediately.

spanish lamb stew with smoked paprika, tomatoes & white beans

5 Tbs. extra-virgin olive oil

2 pounds lamb stew meat, from either the shoulder or leg, cut into 1-inch pieces

1 yellow onion, minced

Kosher salt and freshly ground black pepper

2 Tbs. unbleached all-purpose flour

3 cloves garlic, minced

1½ cups tomatoes, peeled, seeded, and diced (fresh or canned)

1 bay leaf

2 pounds fresh shell beans, shelled, or ¾ cup dried beans or 5 ounces canned

½ pound chorizo, sliced

1 tsp. sweet paprika

½ tsp. pimentón or smoked paprika

2 cloves garlic, sliced

serves 6

ONE OF THE BEST OPTIONS FOR MAKING DINNER ON A BUDGET IS TO use less-expensive cuts of meat. This does not mean compromising on flavor whatsoever, as long as proper cooking techniques are employed. In this dish, lamb stew meat is browned and then simmered over low heat for almost 2 hours. Not only does this method help break down and tenderize an otherwise tough cut of meat, but it also allows the beautiful flavors of the stew to permeate the meat.

My secret to taking this stew to the next level? A spice-infused olive oil drizzled on top. The bold flavors of sweet paprika and pimentón permeate the oil and add feisty Spanish flare to this fabulous stew.

1. In a large, heavy soup pot, warm 2 Tbs. of the oil over medium-high heat. Add the lamb, onions, ½ tsp. salt, and ¼ tsp. pepper and cook, stirring occasionally, until golden on all sides, 8 to 10 minutes. Toss the flour onto the top and stir together. Cook for 2 minutes.

2. Add the minced garlic, tomatoes, bay leaf, and 4 cups of water, and bring to a boil over high heat. Reduce the heat to low and simmer, uncovered, for 1 hour.

3. Add the beans and chorizo and simmer for another 40 minutes. Add additional water if the stew begins to get dry. Taste and adjust with salt if needed.

4. Warm the remaining 3 Tbs. of oil in a frying pan and add the paprika, pimentón, and sliced garlic; cook for 30 seconds but don't let the garlic take on color.

5. To serve, ladle the stew into individual bowls and drizzle with the pimentón and garlic mixture.

- Wine pairing: Tempranillo
- For a first course, toast some slices of rustic bread, rub with garlic, and brush with olive oil. Cup half of a tomato in the palm of your hand. Rub the seeds, pulp, and juice over the bread and sprinkle with kosher salt. If you like, garnish with olives, anchovies, or slices of Serrano ham or prosciutto.

IN THE PANTRY chorizo

Chorizo is a term encompassing several types of pork sausage. In Mexico, chorizo is raw ground pork sausage spiked with vinegar and hot chile peppers, while Spanish chorizo is a cured or smoked sausage made with pimento or dried smoked red peppers.

tuscan pot roast

½ ounce dried porcini mushrooms

1 Tbs. olive oil

3½ pounds beef chuck

Kosher salt and freshly ground black pepper

1 medium yellow onion, finely diced

1 carrot, finely diced

1 stalk celery, finely diced

5 cloves garlic, minced

¼ cup tomato paste

2 tsp. sugar

1 cup full-bodied red wine, such as Chianti or Cabernet Sauvignon

3 cups peeled, seeded, and diced tomatoes (fresh or canned)

serves 6

SERVING SUGGESTIONS

- Wine pairing: Sangiovese or Brunello

- As a side dish, serve soft polenta with lots of Parmigiano-Reggiano added in at the end.

- At the end of the meal, serve a small platter of dates and small chunks of Parmigiano-Reggiano.

IN THIS UPDATED VERSION OF CLASSIC POT ROAST, BEEF CHUCK IS browned then braised in full-bodied red wine. The otherwise tough cut of meat benefits from simmering "low and slow" on the stovetop, becoming so moist and tender that it practically melts in your mouth. Dried porcinis, tomatoes, and tomato paste add deep, rich, savory flavor (also called umami) to the braising liquid, which is then puréed to create a beautiful, silky sauce served atop the succulent beef.

1. Pour 3 cups boiling water over the mushrooms and let stand until the water is cool, 30 minutes.

2. Heat the oil in a large heavy pot over medium heat. Season the meat with salt and pepper and brown the meat, turning occasionally, until golden brown and caramelized on both sides, 20 minutes. Remove the meat from the pot and set aside.

3. Add the onions, carrots, and celery to the pot and cook, stirring occasionally, until the vegetables begin to soften and turn golden, 15 minutes. Strain the porcini and reserve the liquid. Add the reconstituted mushrooms and the garlic to the pot.

4. In a large bowl, stir together the tomato paste, sugar, wine, porcini soaking liquid, and tomatoes. Increase the heat to high under the pot, stir in the tomato mixture, and then add the meat back into the pot. Bring to a boil, reduce the heat to low, and simmer, uncovered, turning the meat occasionally, until the meat is tender, 2½ to 3 hours. To see if the meat is tender, insert a knife or fork into the center of the meat. There should be no resistance and the meat should almost fall apart. If the sauce becomes too thick as it simmers, add water ½ cup at a time.

5. Remove the meat from the pot and cover loosely with foil. Add the sauce to a blender or food mill and purée until smooth. You might have to do this in two batches, and be careful—the sauce is hot, so put a towel over the top of the blender. Taste and season with salt and pepper.

6. Slice the meat into ¼-inch slices and place on a platter. Spoon some of the sauce over the meat. Serve the remainder on the side in a small pitcher.

grilled leg of lamb with lavender salsa verde

4-pound leg of lamb, butterflied and excess fat removed

3 cloves garlic (2 cloves cut into paper-thin slices and 1 clove minced)

6 Tbs. extra-virgin olive oil

Kosher salt and freshly ground black pepper

¾ cup chopped fresh flat-leaf parsley

3 Tbs. chopped fresh chives

1½ Tbs. dried lavender flowers

½ tsp. chopped fresh thyme

½ tsp. chopped fresh oregano

3 Tbs. capers, chopped

1 shallot, minced

1 tsp. lemon zest

3 Tbs. freshly squeezed lemon juice

Lemon wedges, for garnish

serves 6 to 8

SERVING SUGGESTIONS

- Wine pairing: Pinot Noir
- Serve with oven-roasted new potatoes and green beans.

NOTHING BRINGS OUT THE DELICIOUS, DELICATE FLAVOR OF LAMB quite like cooking it over an open flame. Because lamb is naturally more lean than many grilling meats, make sure to coat the lamb well with olive oil to ensure it doesn't stick to your grill.

The amazing flavor combination in the salsa verde was inspired by my cooking classes in the south of France. All of these herbs grow there, and lavender is everywhere. The combination of herbs with the lamb makes this one showstopper of a main course.

1. Prepare an outdoor grill and set the grate 4 inches from the heat source.

2. Lay the leg of lamb flat on the work surface with the exterior of the leg facing down. With the point of a knife, make several incisions in the lamb and insert a slice of garlic into each incision. Brush the outside of the lamb with 2 Tbs. of oil. Season with salt and pepper and set aside.

3. To make the salsa verde, mix together the parsley, chives, lavender, thyme, oregano, capers, shallots, lemon zest, lemon juice, minced garlic, and the remaining 4 Tbs. of olive oil. Season with salt and pepper and set aside.

4. Place the lamb on the grill and grill until golden on one side, 15 minutes. Turn the lamb and continue to grill on the second side until golden and the internal temperature registers 130° to 135°F when an instant-read thermometer is inserted into the thickest part of the lamb. Remove from the grill and set on the work surface for 10 minutes.

5. To serve, slice the lamb into ½-inch slices and place the lamb on a platter. Drizzle with the salsa verde and garnish with lemon wedges.

tortilla soup with pork meatballs, tortillas & cheddar

FOR THE STOCK

10 cups canned chicken stock

1 large yellow onion, diced

1 large carrot, peeled and diced

1 stalk celery, diced

3 cloves garlic, minced

2 large ripe tomatoes, peeled, seeded, and chopped

6 sprigs fresh cilantro, plus leaves for garnish

2 tsp. ground cumin

½ tsp. dried Anaheim chile

½ tsp. pasilla chile

½ tsp. ancho chile

¼ tsp. pimentón or smoked paprika

¼ tsp. dried oregano

2 bay leaves

½ jalapeño, halved and seeded

I USED TO THINK THAT THE ONLY WAY TO MAKE A REALLY GREAT
tasting soup was to use homemade stock. But making stock takes quite a bit of time. That's why I came up with this method for quickly ramping up the flavor of prepared stock. By simmering store-bought stock with a variety of spices and aromatics for just 20 minutes, you create a soup base that you could swear was homemade. Here, tender pork meatballs are baked then added to this fiery, chile-flavored broth along with a variety of vegetables. Garnished with fried tortilla strips, avocado, and Cheddar, this soup packs everything you love about Mexican food into one bowl.

Make the stock
Place the chicken stock, onions, carrots, celery, garlic, tomatoes, cilantro sprigs, cumin, chile powders, pimentón, oregano, bay leaves, and jalapeño in a large soup pot. Bring to a boil, reduce to low, and simmer, uncovered, for 20 minutes.

Make the meatballs and finish the soup
1. Heat the oven to 400°F.

2. While the stock is simmering, in a small bowl, whisk the egg and milk together. Add the breadcrumbs and mix together to moisten the crumbs. Discard any excess liquid. Add the pork, oregano, and cayenne and stir together. Season with 1 tsp. each salt and pepper. Test for flavor by making a patty with a small amount of the mixture. Fry the patty until golden and cooked through. Taste for seasoning and adjust as needed. Form the mixture into ½-inch meatballs and place 1 inch apart on an oiled baking sheet. Bake for 10 minutes.

3. Strain the stock and discard the solids. Place the stock back in the soup pot and add the meatballs, green beans, and carrots and cook until the vegetables are almost tender, 5 minutes. Add the corn and zucchini. Simmer for 5 minutes.

FOR THE MEATBALLS
AND SOUP

1 egg

¼ cup whole milk

3 slices white bread, minced in a
food processor (about 2 cups)

1 pound ground pork

½ tsp. dried oregano

Large pinch cayenne

Kosher salt and freshly ground
black pepper

Vegetable oil, for the
baking sheet

½ pound green beans, ends
removed and cut into
1-inch pieces

2 large carrots, peeled and cut
into ½-inch dice

2 ears of corn, husked and
kernels removed

3 zucchini (about ½ pound), cut
into ½-inch dice

FOR THE GARNISHES

Corn oil, for frying the tortillas

8 corn tortillas, cut into
¼-inch strips

4 ounces sharp Cheddar,
coarsely grated

1 large avocado, diced

serves 6

Make the garnishes and serve

1. In the meantime, heat ½ inch of corn oil in a deep, heavy pan to 375°F.
Add the tortilla strips and cook until crispy, 1 minute. Remove from the pan
and drain on paper towels.

2. To serve, ladle the soup into bowls and garnish with Cheddar and
avocado. Top with tortilla strips and cilantro leaves.

SERVING SUGGESTIONS

- Drink pairing: Ice-cold Mexican beer
- Start the dinner with tortilla chips and
grilled pineapple salsa.

- For dessert, serve rich hot chocolate
with a good dose of añejo tequila and
topped with whipped cream.

IN THE KITCHEN making meatballs

Before forming meatballs, I always
taste the meatball mixture to be
sure the seasoning is just right.
Because the meat shouldn't be
eaten raw, I make a small patty and
cook it in a frying pan until done. Let
it cool and taste for salt and pepper.

To form the meatballs, first
wet your hands so the mixture
won't stick to them, then roll the
meatballs, sizing them according to
the recipe.

Why do I bake meatballs? Doing
so is much quicker than frying them in a pan. Plus, baking them first
helps them hold their shape so they don't fall apart when they're added
to the soup.

metric equivalents

LIQUID/DRY MEASURES

U.S.	METRIC
¼ teaspoon	1.25 milliliters
½ teaspoon	2.5 milliliters
1 teaspoon	5 milliliters
1 tablespoon (3 teaspoons)	15 milliliters
1 fluid ounce (2 tablespoons)	30 milliliters
¼ cup	60 milliliters
⅓ cup	80 milliliters
½ cup	120 milliliters
1 cup	240 milliliters
1 pint (2 cups)	480 milliliters
1 quart (4 cups; 32 ounces)	960 milliliters
1 gallon (4 quarts)	3.84 liters
1 ounce (by weight)	28 grams
1 pound	454 grams
2.2 pounds	1 kilogram

OVEN TEMPERATURES

°F	GAS MARK	°C
250	½	120
275	1	140
300	2	150
325	3	165
350	4	180
375	5	190
400	6	200
425	7	220
450	8	230
475	9	240
500	10	260
550	Broil	290

index

If you like this book, you'll love *Fine Cooking*.

Read *Fine Cooking* Magazine:

Get six idea-filled issues including FREE digital access. Every issue is packed with triple-tested recipes, expert advice, step-by-step techniques – everything for people who love to cook!

Subscribe today at:
FineCooking.com/4Sub

Discover our *Fine Cooking* Online Store:

It's your destination for premium resources from America's best cookbook writers, chefs, and bakers: cookbooks, DVDs, videos, special interest publications, and more.

Visit today at:
FineCooking.com/4More

Get our FREE *Fine Cooking* eNewsletter:

Our *Make It Tonight* weekday email supplies you with no-fail recipes for quick, wholesome meals; our monthly eNewsletter inspires with seasonal recipes, holiday menus, and more.

Sign up, it's free:
FineCooking.com/4Newsletter

Become a CooksClub member

Join to enjoy unlimited online access to member-only content and exclusive benefits, including: recipes, menus, techniques, and videos; our Test Kitchen Hotline; digital issues; monthly giveaways, contests, and special offers.

Discover more information online:
FineCooking.com/4join